THE NEW ART OF
PAPER
FLOWERS

The Complete Guide to Crafting
Gorgeous Crepe Paper Flowers

QUYNH NGUYEN

Blue Star
Press.

To all the flower lovers who have peered into a flower and taken it apart—
examined every little botanical part and wondered how they all fit together—
this book is for you.

"In the cherry blossom's shade there's no such thing as a stranger."
– Kobayashi Issa, Japanese haiku poet

CONTENTS

INTRODUCTION

WELCOME TO THE WORLD OF PAPER FLOWERS, where creativity blossoms and imagination takes flight. I am Quynh Nguyen, the heart behind this book, and I am thrilled to share with you the art that has filled my life for the past decade.

Within these pages, you will find a collection of twenty-five tutorials and five floral projects that reflect not just my craft, but the passion I have for paper flower-making. It is a journey that started by accident, and has become a personal escape, a form of self-care that allows me to recreate the serene beauty of nature with my own hands. Now, I want to extend that joy to you.

Whether you are a seasoned paper florist or a newcomer, I have crafted tutorials to suit every skill level. From the simplicity of an hour-long project to the intricacies of more complex designs that take a bit more time, there is something here for everyone. Before you begin, take time to review the Supplies and Techniques sections, read the tutorial, and gather the supplies listed.

I hope this book becomes a source of inspiration, whether you are crafting to decorate your space, create personalized gifts, or simply for the sheer pleasure of making. Each page is an invitation to experience the quiet joy of creating, a moment of serenity in a busy world. So, gather your materials, find a comfortable spot, and let the delicate petals of paper flowers unfold under your fingertips. Happy making!

– QUYNH

SUPPLIES

You can easily start crafting paper flowers with nothing more than crepe paper, wire, tacky glue, and scissors. The other supplies listed here will elevate your paper flowers to the next level. Feel free to experiment beyond what I recommend. The beautiful thing about paper flowers is that you can make each bloom truly your own. Take a deeper dive into learning about paper flower supplies by referencing my website and other artists' resources.

CREPE PAPER

The first thing people think of when I say "crepe paper" is party streamers made of this beautifully crinkled paper. In fact, it gets its name from its crinkled, fabric-like texture. The many folds pressed into the paper make it easy to shape. It comes packaged in folded sheets or rolls. You will typically need less than one sheet of crepe paper for each tutorial in this book.

German and Italian crepe paper are the types most often used by paper artists because of their consistent high quality. The two key factors to consider when selecting crepe paper are **weight** and **color.**

Manufacturers list paper weight in grams per square meter (gsm or g). A low gsm number means the crepe is lightweight and best suited for fluttery, delicate uses. A high gsm number means the crepe is heavy, thick, and has more stretch. To thicken and strengthen lightweight crepe paper (and to create a two-color effect, if you like) you can layer two sheets together with glue using the laminating technique (page 20). **German doublette crepe paper** comes pre-laminated, made with two sheets already layered together. I recommend these weights of crepe paper:

German crepe paper made by Werola in 48 gsm fine, 60 gsm extra fine, 90 gsm doublette crepe, which is also called double-sided or Gloria, and 160 gsm heavy crepe.

Italian crepe paper made by Cartotecnica Rossi in 40 gsm, 60 gsm, 90 gsm, 140 gsm, and 180 gsm.

All you need to start is a few colors. White crepe is the most versatile and easy to change with coloring mediums (page 11). You will also need a yellow for flower centers and a neutral green for foliage. In the realm of crepe paper, you will find a plethora of basic colors and intermediate shades. Italian crepe papers boast a wider color spectrum and more individual color options than German variants. German doublette (double-sided crepe paper) typically features distinct colors on each side. If you prefer uniformity, consider laminating fine crepe paper to create custom double-sided sheets.

You can add depth to crepe color by layering on coloring mediums like soft pastels, watercolors, gouache, and alcohol markers. It is easy to soften paper colors with color washing (page 25), and color removed from paper in that process can be repurposed as a custom dip-dye (Scrap Crepe Dye, page 25).

> *Note: It takes less than one sheet of crepe paper to make a flower. Have extra sheets on hand if you want to make multiples for a bouquet or Floral Project.*

WIRE

Wire can bend without breaking. It is packaged as floral stem wire and in wire spools; for this book's tutorials, all you need is standard 14" or 18" floral stem wire. Because wires get wrapped together or taped to the main stem, the exact length is not important. I like using standard straight wires, because it takes a little time to straighten spooled wire and measure it to size. So, if I instruct you to cut a wire in half, cutting either a 14" or 18" wire into two 7" or 9" pieces will do the job.

A wire's **gauge** is simply a measure of its weight and thickness; the higher the number, the lighter and thinner the wire; the lower the number, the heavier and thicker the wire. A typical paper flower's stem is 16- or 18-gauge wire. A lightweight flower head sits best on a finer 20- or 22-gauge wire. Small flowers and foliage use lighter 26-, 28-, 30-gauge wire or higher.

bare wire in 16-, 18-, 20-, 22-, 24-, 26-, and 30-gauge;

paper-covered wire in 18-, 20-, 24-, and 26-gauge, in colors like kraft, green, brown, and white;

white wire in 24- and 28-gauge.

Tool Tip: Do not fall into the habit of using your scissors to cut your wires, as it will damage your scissors. I know it can be tempting, but you may regret it in the long term. Use your wire cutter. My favorite is the round wire cutter made by Clauss.

STRUCTURAL MATERIALS

These malleable, supportive supplies help bulk up, sculpt, shape, and arrange crepe paper flowers.

chicken wire, for floral arrangement;

plastic tubing ($^3/_{16}$"), for thickening stems;

kenzan, also known as flower pin frogs or flower frogs, for stabilizing arrangements;

papier-mâché (page 244), for thickening branches and sculpting organic shapes;

polystyrene balls, small, for the core of densely petaled flower heads like ranunculus and poppies;

spun cotton balls, small, for the core of densely petaled flower heads like spray garden roses and dahlias;

modeling clay in white, such as Crayola Model Magic, for creating details like tiny buds, berries, intricate poppy centers, and pollen.

ADHESIVES

Adhesives hold everything together and disappear in your finished work. Similarly, **clear coatings** and **spray treatments** protect paper and make it stronger. These are my go-tos:

floral tape or crepe tape (page 24) in medium green, dark green, white, and clear, for attaching blossoms and leaves and finishing your stems;

Note: *I get a lot of questions about floral tape. What's the go-to tape to buy? My favorite brand of floral tape is Floratape, which you can find at a floral supply shop. Floratape is a superior quality tape that does not rip easily and its glue, when activated, tacks on well. If you cannot find Floratape or if you want to match a specific color, it is quite easy to make your own floral tape out of crepe paper (Crepe Tape, page 24). Make sure to store your tape in a closed container so the glue does not dry out.*

glue gun, optional, for Floral Projects (page 220);

glue stick, for laminating crepe paper;

Mod Podge in matte, typically for petals, and gloss, typically for leaves;

tacky glue, such as Aleene's, for crepe paper and as an all-purpose adhesive;

UV archival spray, clear, for preventing light discoloration.

Convenient products like **fusible webbing** and **adhesive sprays** are reliable backup options. Avoid white school glue (such as Elmer's); a few key differences make tacky glue a far better choice. Tacky glue is thick and viscous, so it grabs onto materials quickly. Plus, it drips less, and it dries faster.

COLORING MEDIUMS

Coloring mediums such as these are ideal for adding color to petals and finished blossoms:

acrylic paint;

alcohol markers, such as Copic Markers, for fine lines;

gouache;

hard pastels;

Scrap Crepe Dye (page 25);

soft pastels, such as PanPastels;

spices, such as ground turmeric or ginger, for creating the look of pollen;

watercolors;

water-based markers, such as Crayola.

Tip: *Alcohol markers dry quickly once exposed to air. They work well for drawing on fine lines, especially those cute pansies' faces.*

TOOLS

Tools like scissors and a ruler are must-haves, and the rest of these come in handy too:

awl or skewer, for curling petals and leaves or making imprints and fine lines;

cosmetic tools, such as foam wedge sponges, thick makeup brushes, or eyeshadow applicators, for applying soft pastels, such as PanPastels, which come in small pans of cake-like pressed powder;

gloves, for coloring crepe paper without staining your hands;

guillotine cutter, optional, great for cutting large amounts of crepe paper in even lines;

needle-nose wire pliers, for bending wires to create your flower or bud's center;

paintbrushes in a variety of sizes: flat brushes for fine lines, round for thick lines and washes;

round wire cutter, such as Clauss, for cutting petal and leaf wires into shorter lengths;

ruler, for measuring paper and wire;

scalloped pinking shears (3 mm), for cutting small petals and sepals for smaller flowers;

scissors, preferably Kai Scissors in 6½" for general cuts and detail work and in 8" for breaking down bigger sheets of paper and cutting through many layers at once.

RESOURCES

Here are some of my favorite places to find crepe paper, craft supplies, tools, and more.

Aleene's Original Glues: aleenes.com

BLICK Art Materials: dickblick.com

Carte Fini: cartefini.com

Cartotecnica Rossi: cartotecnicarossi.it

David Austin Roses: davidaustin.com

David Austin Wedding Roses, Leonora: davidaustin.com/rose/leonora-rose

Etsy: etsy.com

Floral Supply Syndicate: fss.com

Hobby Lobby: hobbylobby.com

JOANN: joann.com

Kai Scissors: kaiscissors.com

Michaels: michaels.com

PanPastel Professional Quality Pastel Colors: panpastel.com

Paper Mart: papermart.com

Rose Mille: rosemille.com

The Stoneground Paint Co: stonegroundpaint.com

Tip: *Online shops like Carte Fini, Paper Mart, and Rose Mille take the mystery out of finding high-quality imported crepe paper. Local craft stores often carry a good variety as well. In fact, you can find a lot of paper flower supplies in the craft and floral sections of hardware stores and general retailers, such as Ace Hardware, Amazon, Daiso, Home Depot, Lowe's, Target, and Walmart.*

TECHNIQUES

These methods and commonly used paper flower terms give you the foundation for making any crepe paper flower.

Accordion Folding is a quick way to cut many layers. Measure the amount specified, and fold with the grains back and forth like the center of an accordion. This keeps every layer the same size and exposes all the folds if they need to be cut. Most of the tutorials will tell you to accordion fold; make sure to fold with the grain, unless told otherwise.

Caring for Paper Flowers: The same qualities that make crepe paper a joy to use also make it susceptible to damage. Avoid direct sunlight, water, jostling, and anything that will smoosh your bloom. The colors of crepe do fade over time, but using high-quality paper, coloring mediums, and UV-resistant spray can mitigate fading.

Curling is a technique most often used for petals, like rose petals. You can use various tools, such as a skewer, slim paint brush, or awl. Something with a pointed end will let you control how tight your curls will be. In a pinch, you can use the back of your scissors to curl.

Cutting works best with sharp scissors that are regularly cleaned and sharpened. If you tend not to measure or cut precisely, cut a bit more than the length given in the instructions; it is better to have a little extra than not enough. When you are done cutting for the day, take a moment to clean your blades, and make sure there is no glue or debris caught between them.

Cupping gives crepe paper a concave shape, most often for petals. Place your thumbs together on top and your index and middle fingers on the back. Pull your fingers out and away from you, while pressing your thumbs into the center. Stop before reaching the edges to avoid overstretching the entire piece.

Cupping Mitered Petals: The crepe paper grains are diagonal instead of up and down. When you stretch the crepe paper, make sure you are pulling the grains apart. Shift your fingers so they are perpendicular to the grains and give a slight stretch.

Cupping Shallow Petals and Deep Petals: Use varying degrees of cupping depending on how concave you want your petals to be. Best practice is to under-cup, because once you stretch out crepe paper, it loses its crepe texture and ability to hold its shape.

Reverse Cupping: Some people find this reverse method easier than cupping; the result is the same, you just need to flip it over afterward. To do reverse cupping, place your thumbs on top of the paper and your index and middle fingers on the back. Gradually push out with your fingers toward you while pressing into the center with your thumbs. Stop before reaching the edges to avoid overstretching the entire piece.

Making Darts is a nifty trick to use when sculpting organic shapes out of paper. Darts reduce paper bulk, and they deepen the cup of any cupped petal or leaf in a natural, curved shape, as in the Double Peony (page 210) and Tulip (page 164).

De-Bulking Darts: Cut a tiny slit or slim wedge ½" into paper.

Cup Deepening Darts: Cut a tiny slit or slim wedge about ½" to 1" into paper.

To secure the darts, use tacky glue to glue the overlap sides of the slit or wedge.

SLIM DARTS

WIDE DARTS

Finding the Paper Grain: The texture, or the grain, of crepe paper gives it its stretch and durability. Understanding grain is critical to knowing the right direction to cut. (See Measuring, page 21.) We cut width measurements against the grain, so the crepe keeps its crinkles—the secret to its strength and durability—and behaves properly, stretching, cupping, and ruffling as needed. To find the grain, follow tutorial instructions and check the templates that show which direction the grain should run.

Tip: Check grain direction and measurements twice before you cut.

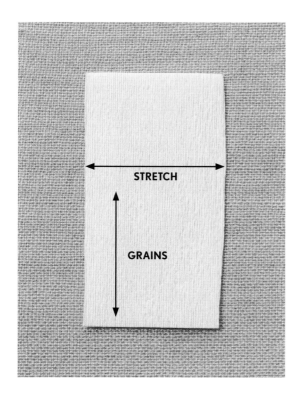

Fringing means making many even, parallel cuts along the paper grain. Use sharp, pointed scissors, such as 6½" Kai sewing scissors. Do not fret over perfection. If your cuts are not as thin as you want, you can always go back and cut them in two or twist to taper them. You can twist fringe individually or accordion fold the whole strip and roll it back and forth between your hands. Fringing is a quick way to create the effect of a pollen-dusted stamen.

FRINGING TO MAKE A STAMEN

Follow your selected flower tutorial's instructions for crepe paper colors and measurements.

Measure and cut against the grain to make two crepe paper strips, typically one short yellow strip (pollen) and one tall white strip (filament). Fold the yellow strip in half lengthwise. Apply a thin line of glue on both of its inner sides.

Fold and glue the yellow strip over the edge of the white strip, making sure it's strongly attached—no open gaps. (When you cut into it to fringe, pollen will fall off if not glued down properly.) Let dry for about five minutes or until no longer damp. Fold up the bottom of the white strip, against the grain (and lengthwise), to line up below the yellow strip; move it higher for shorter filaments or lower for longer filaments. Unfold it, and the crease line will be a guide for even cutting.

To fringe, cut about ¼" to 1" (depending on the flower) from the yellow edge; typically, you will want to keep the pollen tips even. You can cut notches to de-bulk the bottom of the base if it is too bulky. Attach the fringed stamen per the flower tutorial's instructions, and, before the glue dries, apply pressure around the stamen's base; the more you press, the more it will open and bloom.

Tip: If you find it hard to hold the strips together and cut at the same time, consider using a binder clip while you fringe. It will lessen the strain on your hands.

Here's a quick alternative: Try playing with color to make your own pollen layer. Instead of laminating yellow crepe to add pollen, apply yellow color and a little texture to the edges of a single strip of white crepe with a medium yellow alcohol marker, acrylic

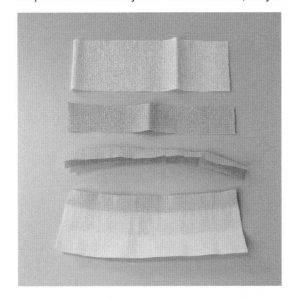

paint, or even spices like turmeric powder to create a pollen-dusted effect. This is quicker and easier on the hands. Be sure that whatever you use is dry before cutting into it.

Gluing requires tacky glue unless otherwise noted. Start with less than you think you need—no more than a few dots or thin lines. Less is more—you can always add more later! Try working in batches, such as applying glue to all the petals for the first row at once. Giving the glue time to dry slightly actually helps it stick faster. You can put a small amount of glue in a bowl when you start a project so that its tackiness increases while you work. To spread glue evenly, apply it with a flat brush.

Tip: If you forget to put on the glue cap and find that it is too thick, add water, a few drops at a time, mixing to achieve a looser glue texture.

Laminating layers of crepe together with glue strengthens thin paper and can be used to craft elements like petals with different colors on each side. Use a flat brush to spread a thin layer of tacky glue on the first paper. With the grain running in the same direction, place the next strip on top. Rub along the grain to stick together. Use any tacky glue that dries clear, like Aleene's. The glue should have a ribbon consistency when it pours; add water to dilute as needed. While tacky glue is my preferred choice, you can also use a glue stick, fusible webbing, or adhesive sprays.

Layering coloring mediums in paper flower-making significantly enhances depth and realism. Begin with a base layer using transparent mediums like watercolors or dyes, setting the tone with soft, diffuse colors ideal for creating natural gradients and shadows on petals and leaves.

After the base layer dries, deepen the hues with PanPastels. These highly pigmented, blendable colors intensify mid-tones and enhance shadows, allowing for layering over lighter shades without covering them, adding crucial volume and dimension. Further refine details using fine brushes or colored pencils to add veining and color breaks, particularly in distinctive patterns like those of pansies, or to highlight petal edges with darker or contrasting hues. This detailed work closely mimics natural floral markings, enhancing the flower's realistic appearance.

Revisit mediums to adjust depth, saturation, or detail, such as adding a final wash with watercolors or highlights with white gel or alcohol pens. This iterative process lets your unique style develop as you build and refine.

Seal your work with a fixative to protect the pigments and prevent smudging. When effectively manipulated, each medium's unique properties elevate the craftsmanship and aesthetic of your paper flowers. Continuously experiment and practice to master color layering, making each creation a showcase of your evolving artistic skill.

Note: When applying wet paint to crepe, some of the crepe color will bleed into the paint, changing the color.

Measuring the right direction is key to success with crepe paper. All measurements are given in inches and in **width x height**. The width typically runs against the grain, meaning it is perpendicular to the grain lines; the height runs with the grain, meaning it is parallel to the grain lines. Cutting width measurements against the grain makes the most of crepe paper's crinkled texture, keeping it stretchy and durable, and able to shape, cup, and ruffle beautifully. Cutting height measurements with the grain adds stability to your paper. So, when measuring, know that the width is how wide your petals and leaves are, and the height is how tall they are. Double check that your measurements and grain direction match tutorial instructions and templates before cutting.

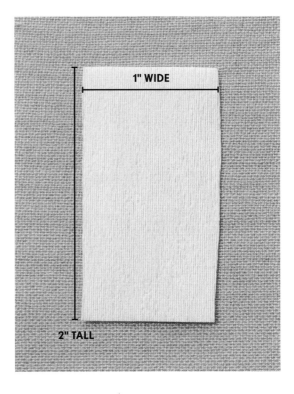

Mitering creates a seam down the center of a piece of paper so that the grain lines run diagonally up and out on both sides like the veins of a leaf. It is used for leaves and some petals, like tulip petals.

Seam Mitering Leaves

With a center seam and natural-looking grain, this technique gives you a structurally strong center, plus a back flap perfect for tucking wires out of sight. Follow your selected flower tutorial's instructions for crepe paper color, measurements, template pattern, and wire (if used).

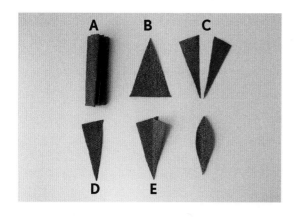

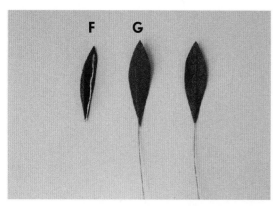

1. **To prepare the crepe paper,** make a strip. Accordion fold it with the grain to the specified width (a). Cut the folds and then cut diagonally from one corner to the opposite corner to form two large triangles (b). Cut the folds of each large triangle to produce smaller triangles (c). Be sure to keep all triangles organized and paired together in their original sets.

2. **To arrange the leaves,** grab two triangle sets and put them together so their longest sides line up (d). Check that their grain forms a V shape, radiating up and out from the center line at a forty-five-degree angle. (This mimics the natural texture and will enhance the realism of each leaf and petal.)

3. **For the seam,** apply a thin line of tacky glue along the longest edge of one triangle in each set. Close the leaf sets so the tops face each other. Press along the glue-lined seams to seal. Let dry. Open each triangle set. Press along the seam, with the extra flap at the back sitting on the right side (e). The paper grain should angle up and away from the center seam in a V shape.

4. **To shape** each mitered leaf or petal, trim with scissors, referring to the template as a visual guide if needed.

5. **Wiring Seam Mitered Leaves:** If the leaf or petal is wired, glue a 26-gauge wire inside the back flap (f), and push it to the inner side (g).

Tip: If you are working with crepe paper that has coat of Mod Podge on it, place the Mod Podge-painted side face up.

Note: When mitering triangles together to make petals and leaves, make sure the triangle pairs always have grain lines radiating out from the center. Sometimes, I form the peace sign or the letter "V" with my fingers to remind myself that the paper grain needs to radiate out.

Overlap Mitering Petals

This technique is typically used for petals because it makes a less bulky seam than seamed mitering.

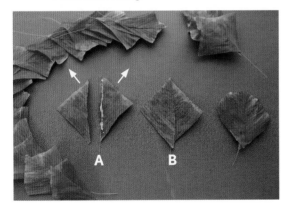

1. **To prepare the paper,** make a crepe paper strip. Accordion fold it with the grain to the specified width. Cut diagonally from corner to corner and cut the folds to create triangles. Cut each triangle in half and keep the sets of triangles paired together.

2. **To arrange the petals,** place halves together facing up in a petal shape. Check that the grain runs out from the center like the letter V (a).

3. **For the overlap,** put a line of tacky glue along the long side of the right triangle. Lift the left triangle over onto the right just enough to cover the glue-lined edge (b). Keep the overlap seam ¼" or less. Check that the paper grain angles up and away.

4. **Wiring Overlap Mitered Petals:** place the stem wire halfway onto the line of tacky glue.

Mod Podging is an informal term for applying Mod Podge, a unique type of water-based glue used as a sealer. It provides a protective—although not waterproof—seal or coating to crepe paper. This coating gives crepe paper extra flexibility and strength, allowing for beautiful petal and leaf movements. Use matte for a flat finish or glossy for some shine. I use a wide, thick brush to apply it evenly, and I clean the brush with hot water as soon as I finish. Before cutting into Mod Podge-painted paper, let it dry—usually one to three hours depending on the humidity of your location. Keep in mind that painting crepe with Mod Podge or anything else makes the color appear slightly darker.

Large-Batch Mod Podging: To avoid having to wait for glue to dry when you want to be crafting, you can prep in advance; paint an entire sheet of crepe paper with a coat of Mod Podge and put it on a wire rack to dry. Store fully dried Mod Podge-painted sheets of crepe paper rolled with parchment paper so they do not stick together.

Ruffling: To add movement to petals, try ruffling the edges. To ruffle or flute your petals, you use a tearing motion without tearing the paper. The folds in the crepe paper help the ruffles hold their shape. My favorite crepe paper for creating the most outstanding ruffles is Italian 90 gsm.

Sealing: If you want to protect your flower, take it outside and—following the manufacturer's precautions and instructions—coat it with UV-resistant clear coating protective spray. Let it dry until you cannot smell the spray before using.

Stretching widens the edge of crepe paper, often the top edge of a petal. Grasp the edge between your fingers and thumbs. Pull gently outward. Repeat as necessary, moving your fingers little by little to get the shape you want, but be cautious: If you overstretch, it can lose its ability to re-crepe.

Taping: When crafting paper flowers, I like to cut and stretch several strips of tape before I need them so I can keep my flower in hand. Floral tape is not sticky to the touch at first. You need to stretch it slightly to activate its stickiness.

Secure the tape and start wrapping: Place the end of the tape at the base of the flower or along the wire you want to cover. Hold it in place with one hand.

Stretch and wrap: Gently pull to stretch the tape as you twist and wrap it around the wire. Stretching is crucial as it activates the adhesive and ensures a tight bind. Overlap the tape as you go to ensure coverage.

Smooth it out: Once you have finished wrapping, press and smooth the tape down to secure it and ensure there are no loose ends.

Crepe tape: You can use any crepe paper to make your own floral tape.

Choose the right crepe paper: Select a crepe paper that matches or complements your flower. It should have a good stretch to it, which is essential for wrapping tightly around stems and other flower parts. Try doublette crepe paper in leaf/moss to match most foliage.

Measure and cut: Cut even strips ¼" or ½" wide against the grain of the crepe paper. This technique will give long, stretchy strips perfect for wrapping around stems or branches. By cutting against the grain, you preserve the crepe's natural elasticity, making the tape more pliable and easier to work with.

Stretch before cutting: For better handling and to maximize the paper's adhesive qualities through stretching, you might lightly stretch the crepe paper before cutting. This pre-stretching aligns with the paper's natural give, making it more pliable and tape-like.

Create your strips: After stretching, lay the crepe paper flat and cut long, thin strips. You can use a ruler and a rotary cutter for precision if you have these tools, or scissors for more freehand cutting.

Use like floral tape: Use these strips as you would use floral tape. Begin by anchoring the end of a strip at the base of the flower or along the wire with a bit of glue. Stretch slightly as you wrap, allowing the crepe paper's texture to grip onto itself and the flower components. Add glue as you wrap.

Extra Coverage: Cut wide 1" to 2" strips for longer stems or branches.

Narrow: Cut slim 1/8" strips for precision work, such as taping delicate stems or tight angles.

Easy Wrapping Crepe Tape: When wrapping multiple stems or branches, cut crepe paper tape on the bias (meaning, cut at a 45-degree angle to the paper grain). This technique allows the tape to flexibly angle up or down, making it easier to cover large surfaces smoothly.

Washing, or color washing, crepe paper is one of the simplest ways to change the color. This might seem counterintuitive, but crepe paper is saturated with so many beautiful colors that are bright and bold. They can be taken out, mixed, and even added back in again.

Washing Crepe to Soften Color: This process mellows color to create beautiful, one-of-a-kind patterns. This can be a useful technique with doublette crepe paper, as it is usually double-sided with two colors and sometimes you want a single color.

Washing Crepe to Make Scrap Crepe Dye: Wear gloves so your hands will not stain with the colors. Have ready some old towels you do not mind getting stained. Cut paper to smaller lengths, so it will be easier to work with. Start with less water than you think you need. When you run the water too long, you wash the colors out and the glue that is holding the paper together. Flip it back and forth to move the colors around inside the folds. When you are ready to experiment more with water washing, add colored scraps of paper into the folds to create or add more colors. Make sure to be delicate when squeezing out the water.

Tip: Save leftover colored water in a jar and use it for your next project!

Drying Washed Crepe: There are many ways to dry washed crepe. You can place it outside in the sun on a rack in the summertime. In colder weather, move the rack indoors near the heat vent to dry. The quickest way for me to dry it is in the microwave. I put the paper on a microwave-safe plate and start with five minutes on medium-high power. Each microwave is different, so make sure to adjust to your microwave's strength. I keep an eye on it in the last minute, checking the dryness and adding more time as needed. You will notice that the fold of paper starts to unfurl as it dries.

THE PARTS OF A FLOWER

The intricate anatomy of a flower plays a crucial role in their formation. When creating paper flowers, understanding the basic structure can help you mimic nature's beauty more accurately.

When making paper flowers, pay attention to the connection points between the stem and leaves, as well as the arrangement of petals around the receptacle. These details will contribute to the realism of your paper flower creation. I highly recommend experimenting with different paper types, colors, and techniques to add your own unique touch to the botanical masterpiece.

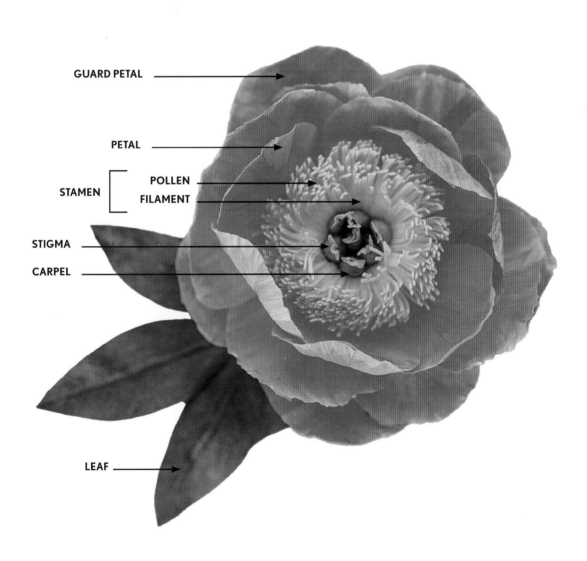

GUARD PETAL

PETAL

STAMEN

POLLEN

FILAMENT

STIGMA

CARPEL

LEAF

THE FLOWERS

Sweet Pea: Raspberry Flake

LEVEL: 3

*The tutorials in this book are rated from level 1 to 10,
with 10 being the most challenging.*

I love sweet peas for their long and elegant lines. They are lovely additions for creating movement in bouquets and centerpieces. The inspiration for this one is the fancy variety Raspberry Flake. For beautifully ruffled petals, we take advantage of the stretchability of 90 gsm Italian crepe paper and use the overlap mitering technique to make them even more ruffly.

Sweet pea flowers flutter together in clusters of five (or more) to a stem. So, for this single sweet pea, we make five flowers. Each flower consists of four petals: a banner petal at the top, two wing petals in the middle, and a smaller keel petal at the bottom. If you would like to accent your sweet pea with leaves and tendrils, follow this tutorial and the Sweet Pea Vine (page 35). Resist the urge to add too many leaves and tendrils—just a few will do. The beauty of the sweet pea is in its delicate blossoms.

When putting a sweet pea stem into a floral arrangement like the Short Modern Monochromatic Floral Arrangement (page 238) or the Floral Headpiece (page 226), focus on the placement of the delicate blooms more than the location of the stem. You can also wire the stem with extra tendrils to create movement in a statement piece.

Sweet Pea: Raspberry Flake

Italian crepe paper in 90 gsm 354 soft pink

German doublette crepe paper in leaf/moss

one 30-gauge wire, cut into five 3½" pieces

one 20-gauge green paper-covered wire, for main stem

tacky glue

floral tape or Crepe Tape (page 24) in leaf/moss

watercolor paint in red

Tools: ruler, scissors, wire cutter, and a fine round brush

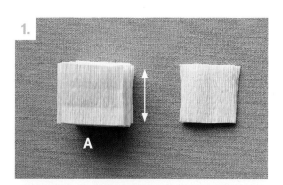

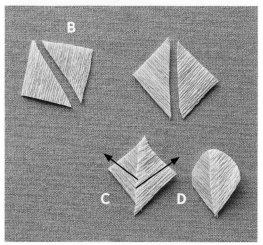

1. **For the petals,** cut with the grain to make one 25" x 1½" strip of soft pink crepe. Accordion fold with the grain every 1¼" (twenty times); cut the folds to make twenty pieces (a). Cut the pieces diagonally into forty triangles (b). Use overlap miter to glue, shape and cup petals as on page 22 (c). Trim triangles into petal shapes using Template: Sweet Pea Petal as a guide (d).

Note: Remember that petals do not have to be perfectly uniform.

2. **For the calyxes,** cut with the grain to make one 4½" x 1¼" strip of leaf/moss doublette crepe (a). Accordion fold it with the grain every ⅞" (five times). Cut five ⅛" wide x ¼" deep darts into the top edge of each piece (b). Cut along the folds to make five pieces (c). Trim the sides at about a 45-degree angle, tapering to the bottom edge (this lessens bulk when added to the blossom) (d).

3. **For the keel petals,** cut with the grain to make five 1¾" x ½" strips of soft pink (a). Stretch them out 100% (b). Going with the grain, fold each strip in half twice. Place a thin line of tacky glue down the middle of a folded strip (c). Fold a corner down along the glue and press to make a triangle. Repeat with the remaining four strips (d). Roll from that triangle all the way across to make a tapered cylinder. Repeat to make five cylinders (e).

4. Fold the five mitered petals in half with the grain. Place lines of glue along the inside folds of the petals and add a 3½" 30-gauge wire down the middle of each.

5. Place the oval cylinder on top of each wire tip and seal the petals closed to make five pod-like keels. Before they dry, slightly bend each keel so they arc back from the wires.

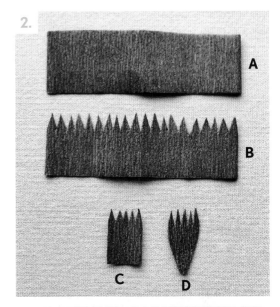

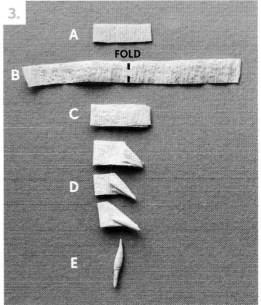

6. **For the wing petals,** fold five mitered petals in half. Place lines of glue along the inside folds of the petals and place a keel in each.

7. **For the banner petals,** place a large dot of tacky glue on the lower right front side of each of the five mitered petals. Layer another petal on top to form a heart shape (a). Repeat to make five heart shapes. Fold each of the five heart shapes in half with the grain (b). Glue along the folds and place the keel and wings set down in the center of each banner petal (c). Let dry, about fifteen minutes.

8. **To add color,** wet a brush, dip it in red watercolor paint, and—testing on scraps first—paint random lines out from the center of each banner petal. Vary the line thickness as you like and do not worry about perfection!

9. **To shape sweet pea blossoms,** slightly spread open the outer edge of banner petals.

10. **Use ruffling** (as on page 24) to add movement and interest to the petal. Do as much or little as looks good to you. Slightly stretch open the middle wing petals. Curl in edges in toward keels.

11. **To assemble,** place a small dot of glue on the lower half of a calyx strip and press around the base of a blossom stem. Repeat with all five.

12. **Use green crepe** to make five 11" x ¼" crepe tape strips Easy Wrapping Crepe Tape (page 25), which is cut on the bias for natural wrapping and draping. Brush a thin 1" line of tacky glue on the end of a strip. Apply crepe tape just above where the calyx ends. Wrap once or twice to secure the tape to the wire.

12.

13. To attach the second blossom to the main 20-gauge wire, bias tape firmly and dot more tacky glue to the tape as you continue past it down the stem. About 1½" down, add the third blossom and wrap tape. Another 1½" down, add the fourth blossom. Wrap tape, and another 2" down, add the fifth blossom.

14. **To finish the stem,** continue taping to the end of the stem wire. Enjoy your sweet peas!

Simple Sweet Pea: If you like, you can choose not to overlap miter the petals. Instead, cut the petals slightly bigger and simply stretch to ruffle them. If adding colorations or strips, consider using a fine-tip brush to paint on the details or an alcohol marker to add those distinctive stripes before putting the petals together. Don't be afraid to try other crepe paper weights, like the German doublette crepe.

Sweet Pea Vine: Use Template: Sweet Pea Leaf, Large and Template: Sweet Pea Leaf, Small (page 248) to create anywhere from two to a dozen leaves. Seam miter them with a 26-gauge wire or lighter. Tape leaves onto the stem in pairs that are 2" to 4" apart. Tape as needed to blend wires into the stem. Tendrils typically appear at the leaf axil between the leaf and the side of the main stem or vine. To add tendrils, wrap to attach 2" to 8" paper-covered wires in medium green, 26-gauge or lighter. Use an awl to curl and taper the ends.

Pansy

One of the many reasons I adore pansies is their versatility. Whether you are extending their stems for a centerpiece or incorporating them into a garden-inspired table setting, these radiant flowers always stand out. Each pansy face is a unique work of art, reflecting the delightful variations found in nature. This individuality allows you to experiment with their robust colors and charming features, ensuring each flower has its own personality. They grow together in lush, vibrant clusters you can tailor to suit a variety of decorative purposes; plus, each pansy's petal is wired with a light gauge so you can manipulate and move the petals to make each pansy unique.

Arranged in a garden-inspired table setting or used to brighten a quiet corner of your home, these pansies add a touch of nature's spontaneity and joy to any space. Their striking appearance and the fun involved in personalizing each bloom make them an essential addition to your crafting repertoire. Crafting each distinct pansy face is not just an artistic endeavor; it is a way to bring the essence of a blooming garden into your projects, with each flower contributing its own unique character to the overall display. This focus on individuality enhances the visual appeal of your creations, making them ideal for displays that capture the vibrant, ever-changing beauty of nature.

Pansy

German doublette crepe paper in goldenrod/
buttercup

Italian crepe paper in 90 gsm 364 sangria

Italian crepe paper in 90 gsm 388 gray green

six 26-gauge wires, cut into five equal parts to
make thirty 3" wires

one 20-gauge wire, for main stem

tacky glue

floral tape or Crepe Tape (page 24) in
medium green

acrylic or gouache paint in dark blue and
yellow ocher

Tools: ruler, scissors, paintbrushes, wire cutter,
needle-nose pliers, awl

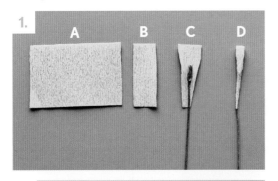

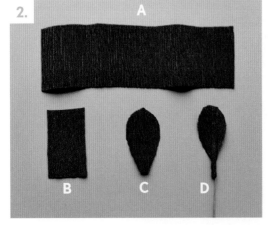

1. **For the pistils,** bend five of the 26-gauge wires about ¼" down, then ¼" down again, in a flat loop. Cut against the grain to make one 2½" x 1" strip of yellow doublette crepe (a). Accordion fold with the grain every ½" (five times) (b). Cut the folds to make five pieces. Use Template: Pansy 2 to trim those five pieces into pistil shapes. Put a thin line of glue on the right sides of all five pistils. Place a bent wire with a flat loop in the middle of each one (c). With an awl, keep the top end open while gluing all five pistils shut (d). Let dry.

2. **For the petals,** cut against the grain to make one 20" x 1½" strip of sangria crepe (a). Accordion fold with the grain every ¾" (twenty-five times). Cut the folds to make twenty-five pieces (b). Use Template: Pansy 1 to cut into twenty-five petals (c).

   Put a line of glue from the middle to the bottom of one petal. Place one 3" piece of 26-gauge wire in the center of the petal about halfway down. Pinch and seal around the wire so it is not seen (d). Repeat to make twenty-five wired petals. Let dry.

Note: *When applying wet paint to crepe, some of the crepe color will bleed into the paint, changing the color. We are creating a dark purple pansy. Red and blue make purple. So, choose a dark blue to apply to red paper.*

3. **To paint the wired petals,** wet the brush and paint so it is thick—not too wet. Leaving two of each group of five petals unpainted, paint the fronts (opposite the side where the wire is glued) of three of the five petals for each flower. Focus the paint on the bottom center of the petal. Draw thin lines radiating from the center. Each petal is unique, so do not worry about uniformity. Let dry.

2.

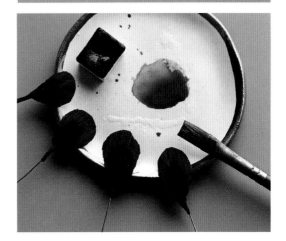

4. **For the sepals,** cut against the grain to make one 5" x 1¾" strip gray-green crepe. Accordion fold with the grain every 1" (five times). Cut along the folds to make five pieces. Use Template: Pansy Sepal 1 to cut those pieces into five sepals.

5. **To assemble the flower heads,** cut a floral tape strip in half so it is narrow, about ¼". With one pistil wire in the center, place three painted petals around the pistil wire with their painted sides facing you; put one to the top left (a), one to the top right (b), and one on the bottom middle (c). Bend the wires as needed.

6. Floral tape this cluster together.

7. Place two unpainted petals (d and e) behind the a and b petals, and tape together.

8. **To shape the petals,** stretch a and b petals about 60%, making sure they sit forward and to the side. Stretch c petal about 80%. Stretch d and e petals about 75% and arrange them to the center and side.

9. Ruffle the petals' tips, especially a and b, as on page 24.

10. **To add color,** if desired, paint thin yellow lines radiating from the center of the pansy to emphasize the pistil.

11. Glue the sepal at the base of the petals.

12. Repeat four more times to make a total of five pansies.

13. **To attach flower heads to the stem,** use gray-green crepe to make Crepe Tape (page 24). Tape a pansy to the 20-gauge wire. Position the next pansy about 1" down the stem and tape. Tape the remaining three pansies together, again positioning each flower 1" below the last. Tape this cluster of three to the main stem. Arrange the stems to lie in a pleasing manner.

Note: Consider creating pansies in various bloom stages and incorporating them into the Floral Headpiece (page 226) to add contrast and interest.

THE NEW ART OF PAPER FLOWERS

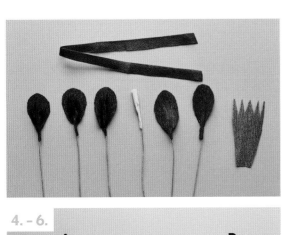

4.

4. – 6.

A   B

C

7.

D   E

A   B

C

8.

11.

SEPAL

13.

Stephanotis

I wish crepe paper were scented, especially for this tiny flower. In nature it exudes a heavenly floral scent, reminiscent of jasmine but distinctly headier, adding a touch of aromatic splendor to any setting. I have been using these charming flowers as small filler blooms in my arrangements and absolutely love the subtle elegance they bring. For those looking to enhance their floral creations, consider incorporating several of these stems into your designs.

In this tutorial, we craft four buds and eight flowering blooms of stephanotis, each capturing the essence of this tropical vine. It is a wonderful substitute for jasmine flowers and offers many decorative possibilities. Use these blooms to add a sophisticated accent to floral arrangements or extend the stems to create striking bouquets. The delicate nature of the stephanotis flowers also makes them particularly stunning in boutonnieres; construct the florets and add the leaves separately for a refined touch.

This bloom is so captivating that you will want to make it repeatedly. Each iteration can be a chance to refine your technique and explore new applications in your floral designs.

German doublette crepe paper in white/white

Italian crepe paper in 90 gsm 365 serpentine

six 26-gauge wires, cut into thirds for eighteen 4½" stems

one 20-gauge wire, optional, for main stem

Mod Podge in matte

tacky glue

floral tape or Crepe Tape (page 24) in dark green

soft pastel, in lime, such as PanPastel in 680.3 bright yellow-green shade

Tools: ruler, scissors, paintbrushes, makeup brush or makeup wedge (or both)

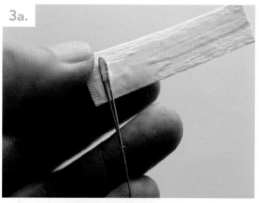

3a.

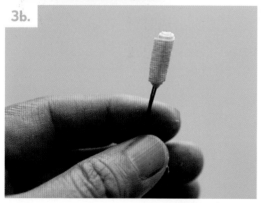

3b.

1. **To prepare Mod Podge-painted crepe,** paint matte Mod Podge onto one 28" x 2" strip of white/white doublette crepe. Let dry, 1 to 3 hours.

2. **For the petals,** cut one 10" x 2" strip of the Mod Podge-painted white/white doublette crepe. Accordion fold with the grain every 1¼" (eight times). Cut the folds to make eight pieces. Use Template: Stephanotis 1 to cut those into eight petals. Cup the tops of the petals. (See Cupping, page 17.)

3. **For the buds:** Use needle-nose pliers to bend the tops of twelve 4½" wires down 1" to build the bulk of the buds. Cut one 12" x 2" strip of the Mod Podge-painted white/white doublette crepe. Accordion fold with the grain every ½" (twenty-four times). Cut the folds to make twenty-four strips. Brush a thin line of tacky

glue on one strip. Place the bent end of a wire at one glue-lined end of it (it doesn't matter which end) (a). Wrap the strip around it (b). Repeat to make twelve wrapped wires. Use Template: Stephanotis 2 to cut the twelve remaining strips into twelve bud petals.

4a.

4. **For the open flowers,** lightly wrap a petal piece around a wrapped wire. Place the top of the wire ¼" below the cut lines of the individual petal (a). Slowly open the petals and position into a five-point star (b). When satisfied with the placement, add a dot of tacky glue and firmly press in place. Wrap the base tightly. Repeat to create eight flowers.

5. **To color,** apply green pastel to the bottom part of the flowers; use a makeup wedge to blend the soft pastel powder into the stem.

4b.

5.

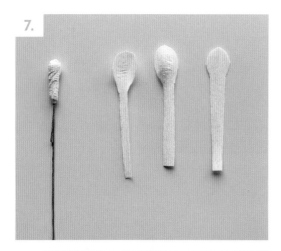

7.

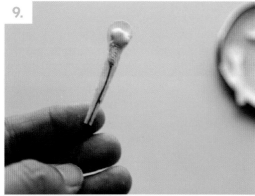

9.

13.

CALYX

14.

THE NEW ART OF PAPER FLOWERS

6. **For the bud petals,** cut one 6" x 1½" strip of Mod Podge-painted white crepe.

7. Accordion fold with the grain every ½" (twelve times). Cut along the folds to make twelve pieces. Use Template: Stephanotis Bud 1 to make twelve petals.

8. Cup the petals (see Cupping, page 17).

9. Place a thin line of tacky glue down the middle of the twelve bud petals on the non-Mod-Podge-painted side.

10. **To attach bud petals to buds,** tacky glue three petals that slightly overlap and cover the core. If you like, you can keep the top part of the petals unglued so it seems like the bud is about to bloom.

11. **To color,** brush the bottom part of the bud with soft pastel in green.

12. **For the calyxes,** cut against the grain to make one 4" x 2" strip serpentine. Stretch out the strip until the 4" strip becomes 9" wide. Accordion fold with the grain every ¾" (twelve times) Cut into twelve pieces.

13. Use Template: Stephanotis Calyx to cut those twelve pieces into calyxes.

14. **To attach to the stem,** tacky glue calyxes 1½" down from the top of the twelve flowers and buds. Make sure each sepal is separated into a five-point star pattern.

15. **For the leaves,** cut one 9" x 3" strip of serpentine. Using 20-gauge wires, accordion fold with the grain every 2¼" (eight times). Use Template: Stephanotis Leaf to cut the leaves. Seam miter to make eight leaves (as on page 22).

16. **To assemble,** gather one cluster of five flowering stephanotis and three buds; make sure they have varying heights (a). Tape the base to hold it together. Place a pair of leaves opposite each other at the base and tape (b). Set aside. Gather a second cluster of the remaining three flowering stephanotis and one bud, again at varying heights (c). Tape them together at the base. Place a pair of leaves opposite each other at the base and tape. Arrange this cluster with the first cluster and tape together.

17. **To finish the foliage and stem:** Tape down another inch or so. Place the last pair of leaves opposite each other, making sure this set sits opposite the earlier set (like a plus sign if viewed from above). Floral tape to finish.

Want a taller piece? Try an **Elongated Stem:** Attach a 20-gauge wire at the base for a long, elegant stem. Wrap with floral tape to finish.

16a.

16b.

16c.

Snowberry Twig

The snowberry, aptly named for its clusters of puffy white fruit, displays beautiful snow-white berries. These branches present a stark contrast against the often-gray winter landscape, providing visual interest when most other plants have faded. As spring appears, tiny leaf buds unfurl into oval-shaped leaves, neatly arranged in pairs along the limbs, heralding the return of life and color. By late summer, the blossoms have transformed into green fruits that gradually ripen into the characteristic white berries.

While real snowberries contain substances that are toxic to dogs, my handcrafted paper and clay versions offer a charming alternative, ideal for incorporating into boutonnieres and wedding bouquets. In fact, I have even created a small, decorative snowberry crown for my beloved fur baby, Butter, allowing her to safely partake in the beauty of these berries without any risk.

This tutorial will guide you through the steps to make a delicate twig that includes eleven paper and clay snowberries, a versatile addition to any creative project. I will also show you techniques for joining these twigs to create larger branches, suitable for more voluminous arrangements or as stand-alone features in floral displays.

German doublette crepe paper in leaf/moss

five 26-gauge brown paper-covered wires, cut into thirds for fifteen 6" stems

modeling clay, such as Crayola Model Magic, in white

foam board or flower frog vase

watercolor paint in light brown or sepia, optional

Tools: ruler, scissors, wire cutter, round paintbrush, awl

2.

UNMITER

MITER

1. **For the leaves,** lay the side of doublette crepe paper you want to be seen facing up; I chose the lighter side (the leaf-colored side). Cut against the grain to make one 24" x 2" strip. Accordion fold with the grain every 1½" (sixteen times). Cut the folds to make seventeen rectangles.

Note: Snowberry leaves do not have to be perfectly shaped or miter. Feel free to make them unmiter and freehand cut them, using the templates as visual references rather than precise pattern templates. Just be sure to check that the grain is going in the right direction.

2. **To shape the leaves,** cut the doublette rectangles into sixteen leaf shapes using the following templates: Make eight of Template: Snowberry Leaf 1, four of Template: Snowberry Leaf 2, and four of Template: Snowberry Leaf 3. Put all sixteen leaves together by seam mitering (page 22) without wiring the leaves; just glue the flap closed where the wire would normally go.

3. **For the berries,** ready a piece of foam board to hold the berry sticks upright to dry without touching each other.

4. Put a bit of tacky glue into a small, shallow dish to dry a little while you are rolling the berries.

   Note: Not all berries are nice and round— some look like tiny pumpkins, and some look like squashed balls. Do not make the snowberries too perfect! Make various sizes to add visual interest to your twig.

5. **To shape the berries,** roll them from clay; pinch off a small pea-size bit and place it in your palm. With three fingers, roll it into a smooth ball, and repeat to make eleven berries that are $\frac{1}{25}$" to $\frac{1}{2}$" across.

6. With the ball on the flat of your palm, dab a bit of tacky glue on the end of a 6" wire stem and insert into the berry. To add details, try these techniques.

   Regular Berry: Push the wire in until you feel it on the other side. Stop and carefully push it out slightly until you can see the wire through the clay, but it has not pierced the skin.

   Dimpled Berry: When you feel the wire end touch your palm, stop, and carefully push it out slightly until you can see the wire, but it has not pierced the skin. To form the dimple, pull the wire back inward into the ball. The glue from the wire will grab the clay and pull some inward forming a cute little dimple.

5.

6.
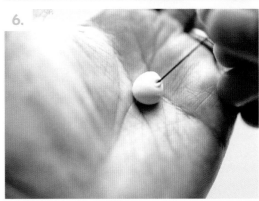

6.
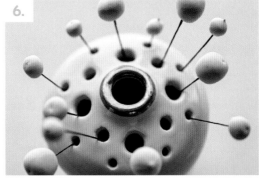

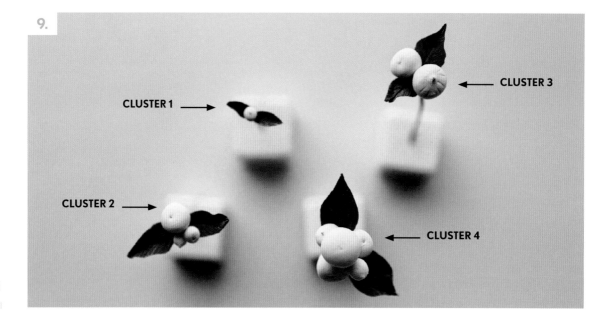

CLUSTER 1

CLUSTER 3

CLUSTER 2

CLUSTER 4

7. **Add texture** to about seven of the berries. Many snowberries have slight grooves like pumpkins. To create this effect, gently press a wire into the side to make a light impression.

Note: You can dry the berries overnight until hardened, but it is not necessary. Just be extra cautious when placing undried berries next to each other. They can stick together and pulling them apart will ruin the shape and details.

8. **To nestle the berries,** put one berry in the center, and place another berry slightly below it. If you turn the piece over, you can more easily see the gaps and places where you may want to put the next berry.

9. **To make clusters of berries and leaves,** arrange them into little groups. Mix up the combos to create various looks. Bend the berries to nestle them together more easily.

Remember that snowberry leaves sit opposite each other in pairs, so keep sets of leaves together. These are the combinations of berries and leaves I like to make:

Cluster 1: one small berry + two leaves patterned after Template: Snowberry Leaf 3;

Cluster 2: two small berries + one medium berry + two leaves patterned after Template: Snowberry Leaf 2;

Cluster 3: two medium berries + two leaves patterned after Template: Snowberry Leaf 1;

Cluster 4: one small berry + two medium berries + two large berries + two leaves patterned after Template: Snowberry Leaf 1.

10. **To assemble the clusters,** dab a bit of glue along the wire stems. Use less glue than you think you need. I also recommend keeping a damp cloth nearby to help clean your fingers. Arrange the wires to form a naturally rounded stem.

11. **To assemble the clusters into stems:** Use the leaves to help hold the stems together. Add a tiny dot of glue to the base of the berry cluster and place two leaves opposite each other. To cup the leaves while placing them, pinch the top part of the leaf in half inward and push the leaf toward the berry.

   Note: To create a more weathered look, lightly wash the berries with light brown or sepia watercolor. If the coloring is too dark, wet your fingertips and rub the color away. (Less is more.)

12. **To assemble the clusters into a bigger twig:** Start with the largest cluster. Move down the large cluster stem about 1" and place a small cluster. Once you are happy with the placement, dab some glue and adhere to the main stem. Right where the stems meet, add two leaves opposite each other. This will give extra strength and hide imperfections. Glue the third cluster slightly below the second, again adding two more leaves where they meet. Add the final stem a little lower and add leaves. Check that the stem does not have any gaps. Trim the uneven wires if this is your finished piece. If adding this twig to a bigger piece, do not trim off the uneven wires at the end. They can help blend the twig into the bigger branch.

Ranunculus

When you look at a ranunculus petal, you will notice that it is not a solid color. The flower glows with the interplay of complementary colors that make the flower shine. I use soft pastels to give petals a subtle ombre effect. When you put all the ombre petals together around the center, which consists of the pistil and stamens—that is when the magic happens. Remember a little soft pastel goes a long way. Make sure to do a test swatch on a sheet of paper before applying it to your crepe paper. I love using a cheap, thick makeup brush to blend the pressed powder of soft pastels (like PanPastel) into paper. The first swipe is usually the most pigmented, so I tend to do that first swipe on a scrap of paper or paper towel before coloring my working crepe paper. Some helpful tools for soft pastels include a cheap, lush makeup brush, a disposable eyeshadow applicator, and a simple makeup wedge sponge. These items are affordable and highly effective for blending and applying delicate pastel colors. You can find all these tools at a dollar store. Their versatility and ease of use make them ideal for achieving smooth, even coverage and precise shading in your paper flower projects. Also feel free to experiment with other color mediums, such as watercolor.

Ranunculus

German doublette crepe paper in white/white

German doublette crepe paper in leaf/moss

one 18-gauge wire

one 1" polystyrene ball, cut in half

watercolor paint in black and green

soft pastels in complementary colors, such as PanPastels in 680.3 bright yellow-green shade, 740.9 burnt sienna tint, 340.8 permanent red tint

tacky glue

medium green floral tape or Crepe Tape (page 24)

Tools: awl, ruler, scissors, wire cutter, paintbrushes, makeup wedge sponge, makeup brush

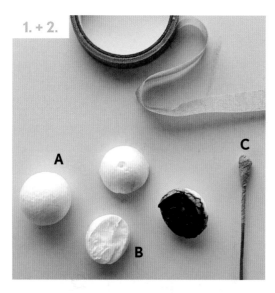

1. + 2.

A

B

C

3.

1. **To prepare the core,** use your scissors to cut the polystyrene ball in half (a). (Set aside half for a future project, such as another ranunculus.) Poke a hole into the center of the domed side with an awl. Wet a paintbrush and mix black watercolor into green to create dark green and paint the flat side but not the domed side (b). Let dry.

2. Wrap floral tape around one end of the 18-gauge wire to make a bulbous end (c). Place a bit of tacky glue in the center of the painted side of the core.

3. Insert the stem (the non-bulbous end of the 18-gauge wire) through the tacky glue into the center of the painted side of the core; push it through until the tape-wrapped bulbous end is nestled tightly in the center of the painted core, and the stem wire end pokes out through the domed bottom side.

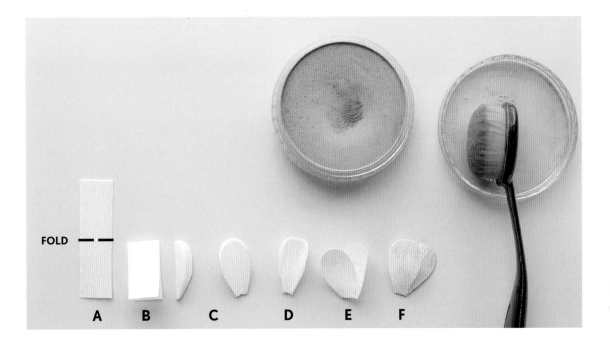

FOLD

A   B   C   D   E   F

4. **For the inner petals,** cut one 3" x 2" strip of white/white doublette. Accordion fold with the grain every ½" (six times). Cut the folds to make six pieces (a). Fold all six pieces in half (b).

5. Making sure to place the template on the fold to keep each pair of petals attached at the bottom, use Template: Ranunculus 1 to cut the six folded pieces into six petal sets (c).

6. Deeply cup the petals (d). Open and fan them out about ¼" (e). Lightly color the top third of each petal with soft pastel in bright yellow; use your fingers or a makeup wedge to rub color into the crepe with an ombre effect (f).

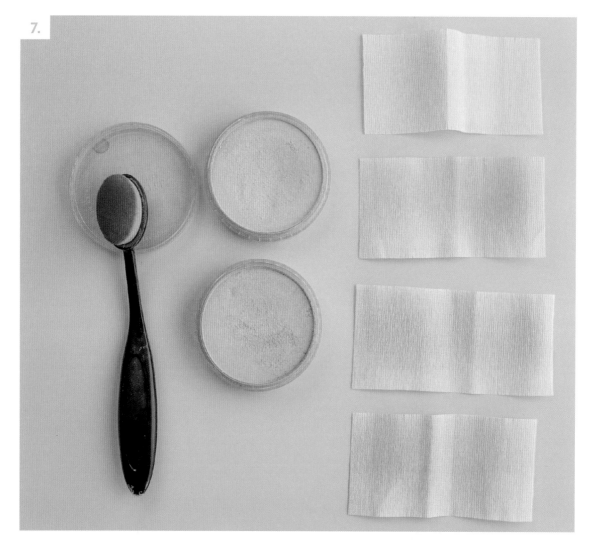

SMALL

MEDIUM

LARGE

7. **For the outer petals,** cut against the grain to make three strips of white/white doublette crepe in **small:** 12" x 2", **medium:** 36" x 2", and **large:** 11¼" x 2". Color all three strips, using a makeup brush to apply burnt sienna and red soft pastels in the middle of each strip and then blending out the colors to the end; create a mix of light and dark patches for a more interesting bloom. Blend and rub until there is no loose powder.

8. **For the small petals,** using the ombre-colored 12" x 2" strip of white/white doublette, accordion fold with the grain every ¾" (sixteen times). Cut the folds to make sixteen pieces. Use Template: Ranunculus 2 to cut them into sixteen petals. Deeply cup with the colored side facing out. (See Cupping, page 17).

9. **For the medium petals,** accordion fold the ombre-colored 36" x 2" strip of white/white doublette crepe with the grain every 1" (thirty-six times). Cut the folds to make thirty-six pieces. Use Template: Ranunculus 3 to cut out thirty-six petals. Cup with the colored side facing out.

10. **For the large petals,** accordion fold the ombre-colored 11¼" x 2" strip of white/white doublette crepe with the grain every 1¼" (nine times). Cut the folds to make nine pieces. Use Template: Ranunculus 4 to cut out nine petals. Slightly cup the middle and top portion of each large petal on the non-colored side.

11. **For the sepals,** cut against the grain to make one 4" x 2" strip of leaf/moss doublette crepe. Accordion fold with the grain every ¾" (five times). Cut the folds to make five pieces. Use Template: Ranunculus Sepal to cut those pieces into five sepals. Cup deeply.

12a.

12b. + 12c.

12d.

12e. + 12f.

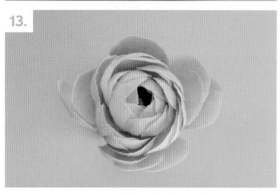

13.

14.

12. To attach the inner petals, tacky glue them close together and equally spaced around the center, overlapping slightly like a fan (a). The tops of the petals will sit above the center. Glue five small petals slightly above the inner petals, making sure to overlap as you glue around the center (b). With the next three small petals, create a triangular set and glue where you ended the last row (c). Make another triangular set and glue a few spaces over, purposely creating a gap (d). Move over a few more spaces and add another triangular set (e). Glue the remaining two small petals in a gap, slightly overlapping one of the petals (f).

Note: For the next several rows of petals, follow these rules: Go clockwise or counter-clockwise, but always go one way, with one exception—sometimes you may want to echo your petals. Echoing means breaking the pattern and reversing one or two petals. This tells a visual story; it makes the eye stop and look instead of just gazing over the flower.

13. To attach the medium petals, pick a gap and start one round of petals moving in the main direction. Make sure to overlap the petals and go all the way around. Create an echo. Look for gaps. Fill in with more echoes to use the remaining medium petals.

14. To attach the large petals, place five large petals evenly around the stem. Fill in gaps with the remaining four large petals.

15. To finish the foliage, tacky glue the five sepals equally around the base in a star pattern. Floral tape the stem. Use a UV-protection spray (page 24) to seal the soft pastel color.

Italian Butterfly Ranunculus

LEVEL: 6

These graceful blooms have iridescent petals that flutter just like the real flower. To create these, I Mod Podge and paint the petals to give extra flexibility without making the paper too stiff. You can use a wire as light as 24-gauge to help these blooms flutter even more like butterflies. The finished flower measures around 3" or less, a dainty bloom perfect to float high in floral arrangements. Consider using these blooms to help create airy arrangements that give the illusion of movement and make them in different colors. Some of the most common colors include shades of pink, yellow, orange, red, and white. Check out my floral wear project, where I changed the color of these fun blooms to pink in various blooming stages and used the poppy leaves as my foliage and the snowberries as my accent pieces to fill in the space and shape the floral wear.

German doublette crepe paper in white/white

German doublette crepe paper in leaf/moss

Italian crepe paper in 90 gsm 357 brown

Italian crepe paper in 180 gsm 567 twig

Italian crepe paper in 90 gsm 376 yellow mustard

one 22-gauge wire, for the main stem

tacky glue and glue stick

Mod Podge in matte

floral tape or Crepe Tape (page 24) in leaf/moss

watercolor paint in orange and yellow

Tools: ruler, scissors, awl, paintbrushes

2.

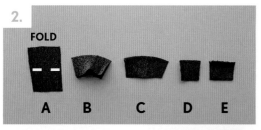

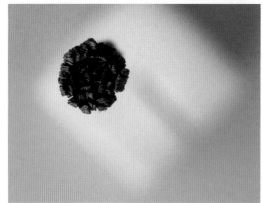

1. **To prepare the Mod Podge-painted paper,** cut against the grain to make one 16" x 2" strip of white/white doublette crepe. Paint one side with matte Mod Podge. Let dry, 1 to 3 hours.

   Note: See Large-Batch Mod Podging (page 23) about prepping and storing larger sheets of gloss and matte crepe for later use.

2. **For the inner center,** cut against the grain to make one 3" x 2" strip of brown crepe (a). Fold the strip in half so it is 1½" x 1" (b). Run the glue stick along the bottom half, then fold in half with the grain to laminate shut (c).

3. Fringe as on page 19, making cuts ⅛" apart and ¼" long into the folded edge (d). Curl the fringe with an awl (e).

4. **To attach the inner center,** apply a thin line of tacky glue along the base of the curled fringe strip. To attach it to the top of the 22-gauge

wire, press firmly against the wire and wrap tightly; the wire should not be seen, but hidden just below the fringed top by about ⅛". Push the fringe down with your thumb to create a tight, round center.

5. **For the outer center,** cut against the grain to make one 3½" x 1½" strip of twig-colored crepe (a). Fold the stretched strip in half against the grain (b). Stretch the strip to about 8" (c).

6. Cut with the grain to make one ¼" x 8" strip of yellow crepe. Twist this yellow strip into a tight rope (d).

7. Put one line of glue into the middle of the open fold in the twig-colored strip. Place the twisted yellow strip in the fold and press closed. Push the twisted strip to the top of the fold so there are no gaps (e).

Note: Do not wait for the glue to dry before fringing. It is easier to cut into a laminated strip before the glue hardens.

8. Fringe the yellow strip, making cuts ⅛" apart and ¼" down. Fold the fringed strip in half and glue sides together.

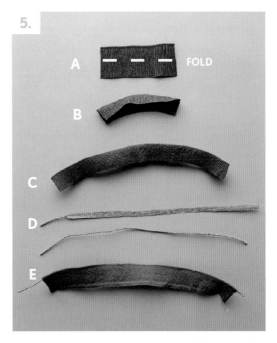

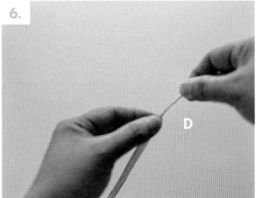

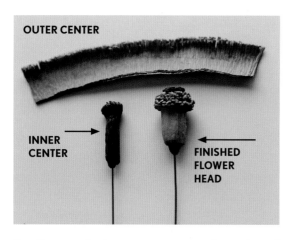

OUTER CENTER

INNER CENTER

FINISHED FLOWER HEAD

9. **To attach the outer center,** place a line of glue on the bottom half of the strip and wrap around the inner center. Place just below the inner center. Each layer as you wrap should be just below the last.

10. Press the bottom part firmly to the stem to make sure the center is tight and firm.

Note: When painting watercolor on crepe paper, less is better. You can always add more color later but cannot take it away without the risk of the doublette crepe layers coming unglued.

11. **For the watercolor-painted petals,** use the 16" x 2" strip of Mod Podge-painted white/white doublette crepe. Accordion fold with the grain every 1" (sixteen times). Cut the folds to make sixteen pieces. Use Template: Italian Butterfly Ranunculus to cut those pieces into sixteen petals. Wet watercolor and combine yellow with just a touch of orange, making one pool of light yellow, one pool of medium yellow, and one pool of slightly darker yellow. Start at the base of each petal and, going with the grain,

paint with upward strokes to color the Mod Podge-painted sides of the petals (but leave the stems white); focus on the border and the bottom third, leaving the top and middle of each petal with less color. Flip over and watercolor the other side, using less paint than before. Blot any excess water with your paper towel. Do not worry if the petals curl; after they dry you can easily reshape them. Let dry.

12. Lay out watercolor-painted petals with the shiny Mod Podge-painted side on top. Cut the smallest petal into three narrow petals. Round their tops, then curl them around an awl so you have three narrow, unfurling petals.

13. For the remaining watercolor-painted petals, place your fingers on the top of the petal and gently stretch. Slowly move down, stretching the sides. Slightly cup the centers.

14. **To attach petals to the flower head,** tacky glue the three unfurling petals evenly around the center, their bases lined up with the base of the center.

15. Place the remaining petals in loose rows around the unfurling petals at the center. There should be a bit of space between each layer. Place any extra petals into visible gaps in the last row.

16. **For the sepals,** cut against the grain to make one 3" x 1½" strip of leaf/moss doublette crepe. Accordion fold with the grain every ½" (six times). Cut the folds to make six pieces. Use Template: Italian Butterfly Ranunculus Sepal to cut out six sepals.

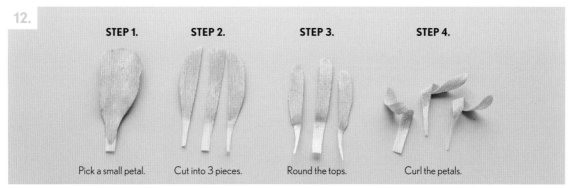

12.

STEP 1.

Pick a small petal.

STEP 2.

Cut into 3 pieces.

STEP 3.

Round the tops.

STEP 4.

Curl the petals.

13.

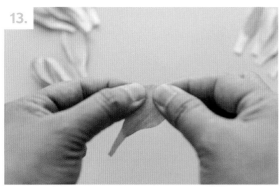

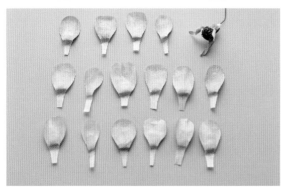

14.

15.

16

18.

19.

17. **To shape,** cup each sepal deeply on the darker side. Dot the darker side with tacky glue.

18. **To attach the sepals to the flower head:** Press to attach three of the sepals around the base of the petals in a triangle pattern. Attach the remaining three in the gaps of the first three.

19. **For the stem,** wrap with floral tape to finish the bloom.

Foxglove

LEVEL: 6

Crafting this classic cottage garden flower's many tubular florets can be meticulous but rewarding. Each individual floret plays a pivotal role in contributing to the overall elegance and distinctive appearance of the foxglove, underscoring the importance of patience and attention to detail during the crafting process. Although the pistil and stamen may not be visible to the casual observer, their intricate construction is crucial, adding significant depth and authenticity to each bloom.

Dive deep into the artistic process of painting the characteristic dots on each floret. Rather than simply applying dots, challenge yourself to create oval shapes or embrace slightly irregular patterns. Allow the dots to occasionally overlap, which mirrors the natural variation in real foxglove flowers. This approach adds a dynamic texture to the flower and makes each piece uniquely captivating.

Take your time and savor the process. Allow yourself to be immersed in creativity, and let this mindful approach not only enhance the visual appeal of your foxglove but also enrich your overall crafting experience.

Foxglove

German doublette crepe paper in white/
white

German doublette crepe paper in
goldenrod/buttercup

German doublette crepe paper in pink/berry

Italian crepe paper in 90 gsm 375 parakeet

eight 26-gauge wires cut into four equal
parts, for 32 wires about 4 ½" each

one 18-gauge wire, for main stem

tacky glue

floral tape or Crepe Tape (page 24)
in medium green

acrylic or gouache paint in white and
dark pink

Tools: awl, ruler, scissors, paintbrush, wire
cutter, needle-nose pliers

1a.

1b.

1. **For the pistils,** cut against the grain to make
one 6" x 2½" strip of white/white doublette
crepe. Accordion fold with the grain every
¼" (twenty-four times). Cut the folds to make
twenty-four pieces and use Template: Foxglove
Pistil to cut those pieces into twenty-four pistils.
Dot tacky glue to put one 4½" wire in the middle
of a pistil, leaving a ½" gap from the top (a); as
you close it, use an awl to keep the top rounded
open (b). Repeat to make twenty-four. Let dry.

2. **For the stamen,** cut against the grain to make two 4" x 2" strips of goldenrod/buttercup doublette crepe. Fold each strip in half against the grain, the darker yellow (buttercup) facing out. Cut against the grain to make two 4" x 2" strips of white/white doublette crepe (b).

Note: Follow the instructions for Fringing to Make a Stamen (page 19), cutting as narrowly as possible, at most 1/16" wide. Fringe to make stamens, cutting down about 1¼" from the yellow edge.

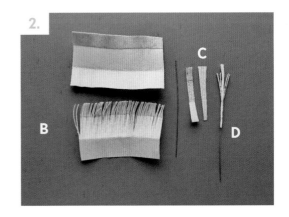

Count four individual filaments of the fringe and cut to make a segment (c). Repeat to make twenty-four stamen segments. Wrap and glue four stamen segments around and ½" down from the top of each pistil (d). Let dry.

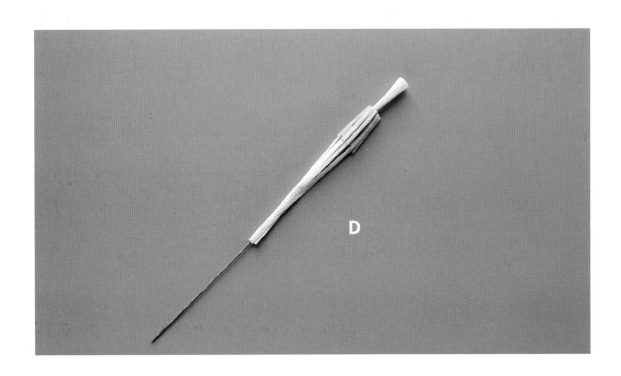

5.

TOP PETAL

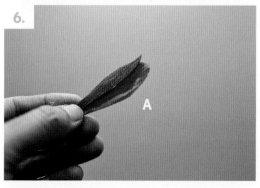

6.

A

3. **For the sepals,** cut one 30" x 1¾" strip of parakeet crepe. Accordion fold with the grain every 1" (thirty times). Cut the folds into thirty pieces. Use Template: Foxglove Sepal 1 to cut the pieces into thirty sepals.

4. **For the bud blossoms' top petals,** cut one 9" x 2" strip of pink/berry doublette crepe. Accordion fold with the grain every ¾" (twelve times). Cut the folds into twelve pieces. Set aside six pieces and use Template: Foxglove Bud 1 to cut the others into six top petals.

5. **To shape the top petals,** hold one with the lighter pink side facing you, and cup the top third of it (for more, see Cupping, page 17). Repeat, cupping the remaining top petals. Use an awl to curl the opening lip of each cupped top petal slightly downward and inward. Put one thin line of glue on the bottom half of all six cupped and curled top petals. Place one 26-gauge wire on each of these glue lines.

6. **For the bud blossom's bottom petals,** use Template: Foxglove Bud 2 to cut six bottom petals from the remaining six pieces of pink/berry doublette crepe. Cup each bottom petal down the center. Use an awl to curl the opening lip of each bottom petal slightly upward and inward. Put a thin line of glue down both sides of each bottom petal (a). Place a top petal onto each glue-lined bottom petal to make six cylindrical bud blossoms. Glue sepals around the base of each one.

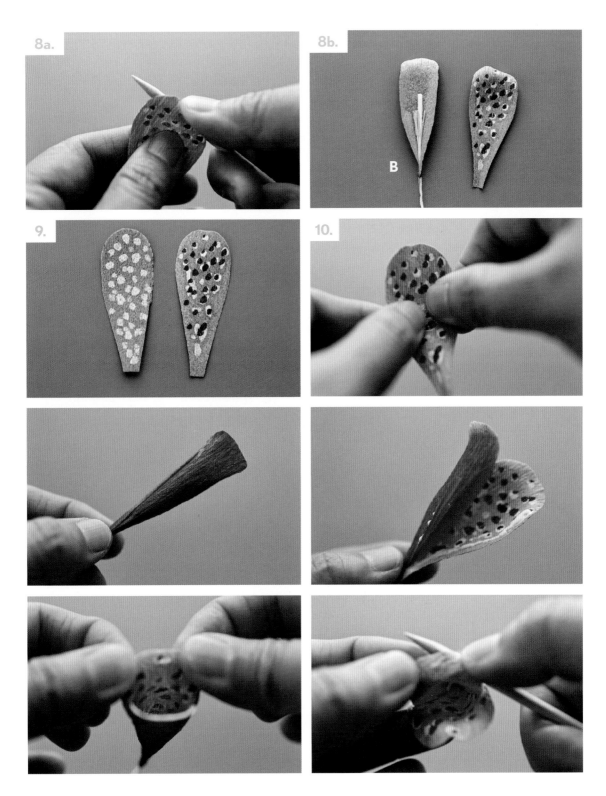

7. **For the blossoms' top petals,** cut against the grain to make one 48" x 2½" strip of pink/berry doublette crepe. Accordion fold with the grain every 1" (forty-eight times). Cut the folds to make forty-eight pieces. Set aside half (twenty-four pieces). Use Template: Foxglove 1 to cut the rest into twenty-four top petals.

8. **To shape the top petals,** with the lighter pink side facing you, cup the top third of each one. Use an awl to curl the opening lip upward and outward (a). Put a thin line of glue in the bottom half of each top petal. Place one stamen wire onto each line of glue, with the tip of the pistil in the middle of each one (b).

9. **For the blossom's bottom petals,** use Template: Foxglove 2 to cut twenty-four bottom petals out of the remaining 1" pieces of pink/berry doublette crepe. Paint these bottom petals with random white dots, then add dark pink dots. Be as random as possible—have fun and make each petal unique. Let dry.

   Note: Less glue is better than more—especially when gluing delicate foxglove petals together.

10. **To shape the painted bottom petals,** cup each one down the center. Use an awl to curl the opening lip of each bottom petal upward and outward, exposing more of the dots. Place a thin line of glue down both sides of the bottom petals. Glue one bottom petal to each top petal. Glue the sepals around each base to complete all twenty-four blossoms; before the glue dries,

use needle-nose pliers to bend the wires at the base of each blossom into a small, ~½" loop to make assembly easier later.

11. **To attach petals on the flower head,** prepare several narrow, ¼" pieces of floral tape to have ready. To make foxglove flowers hang naturally, place them at a 75-degree angle (rather than a downward angle). They may stick out at first, and you will adjust them later. Remember, when adding blossoms, look for gaps to fill. Tape the tiny stems and blossoms together using these rows as a guide.

> **Row 1:** Start floral taping and add one bud. Tape two bud blossoms side by side to the first one.
>
> **Row 2:** Add three bud blossoms.
>
> **Row 3:** Tape two blossoms.
>
> **Row 4:** Tape the 18-gauge stem plus two more blossoms.
>
> **Row 5:** Tape three blossoms.
>
> **Row 6:** Tape three blossoms.
>
> **Row 7:** Tape four blossoms.
>
> **Row 8:** Tape four blossoms.
>
> **Row 9:** Tape three blossoms.
>
> **Row 10:** Tape three blossoms.

To finish the stem, finish floral taping the rest of the stem, and you are done!

11.

Note: You can use scissors to quickly estimate small measurements. Floral tape is usually ½" wide. So, to quickly cut narrow, ~¼" tape strips like the ones needed for Foxglove stems, try cutting a piece of floral tape, folding it until it fits easily under your scissors, and then cutting along the fold into strips.

Lilac Sprig: Purple Sensation

Create the stunning Purple Sensation Lilac, a fun floral display featuring delicate purple petals, each gracefully outlined in white. In this tutorial, you will master making buds from modeling clay. You will appreciate how effortlessly the clay molds and absorbs color, making it a pleasure to work with.

Constructing this flowering stem is a labor of love, as the more blossoms and buds you craft, the fuller and more lifelike your lilac will appear. Although the process is time-consuming, the result is undoubtedly worth every minute. For this project, I highly recommend using sharp-pointed scissors, such as the Kai 6½" scissors, which are ideal for precisely cutting the tiny, intricate petals needed for these small blossoms. Take your time with each step, from cutting to painting the petals, and you'll discover that your efficiency and speed will improve significantly with practice.

The meticulousness needed for this project not only enhances the beauty of each bloom but also deepens your own skills and satisfaction. Have fun with this project and make them in whites, blues, pinks, and even magentas.

Lilac Sprig: Purple Sensation

Italian crepe paper in 90 gsm 395 blue mussel

twelve 26-gauge wires, cut into four equal lengths to make forty-eight 4 ½" stems (twelve for buds and thirty-six for blossoms)

one 18-gauge wire, for the main stem

tacky glue

floral tape or Crepe Tape (page 24) in medium green

modeling clay, such as Crayola Model Magic, in white

gouache paint in white, magenta/dark purple, and blue/dark purple (Stone Ground Paint in beetroot purple and iris pictured here)

Tools: ruler, scissors, paintbrushes, fine paintbrush, needle-nose pliers

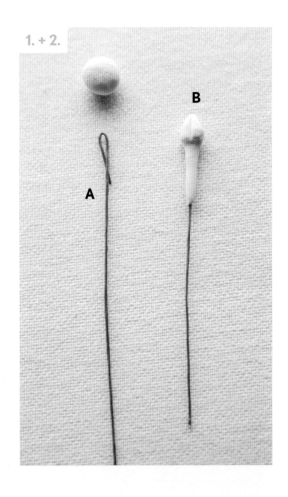

1. + 2.

A

B

1. **To prepare a base** for the buds and blossoms, use needle-nose pliers to bend each tip of the 4½" wires down ½" into a flat loop (a).

2. **For the buds,** roll a small pinch of modeling clay into a ball. Flatten the clay and wrap it around the bent end of a 4½" wire to create a bulbous end (b). Gently pull excess clay down the stem about 1". Remove any extra clay by sliding down the stem. With scissors, use the motion of cutting to indent the bud part in a plus sign shape for the bud's inner petals; do not cut through the clay (c). Repeat for a total of twelve buds. Once the buds are halfway dry, you can paint them.

Note: You can use dye extracted from crepe paper to make a watercolor-like color wash in custom colors. Or mix it into paint for one-of-a-kind hues. Simply soak a bit of purple crepe in water to extract the ink (see Scrap Crepe Dye, page 25).

3. **To paint the buds,** prepare small pools of various shades of purple on your paint palette for bud highlights and shadows. Start by mixing a touch of the blue-toned paint with more of the magenta-toned to create a purple that is a close (but not exact!) match with the crepe. Wash the whole bud in a purple shade. Use the darker colors at the base for shadows and add lighter purples at the tip of the bud for highlights. Set aside to dry, making sure the buds do not touch each other and stick together.

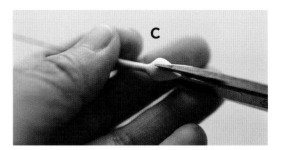

4. **For the stamens,** cut against the grain to make one 59" x ½" strip of blue mussel crepe (I use a guillotine cutter to chop off the top of an entire roll; it is the perfect length—you will have extra paper to create a fuller bloom look). Stretch out the strip 100%. Accordion fold with the grain every 1½" (36 times). Cut along the folds to create thirty-six short strips. Brush a light coat of tacky glue onto a short strip and wrap around the bent part of a 26-gauge wire to create a stamen. Repeat for a total of thirty-six stamens (or cut more paper to create seventy-two blossom wires for a fuller bloom).

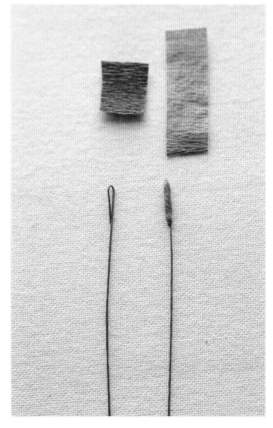

5.

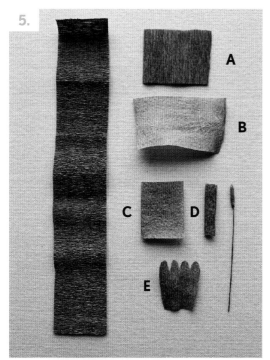

A

B

C   D

E

F

6.

the following steps to create thirty-six blossom stems: Brush a light coat of glue over half of a strip and fold to glue closed (c). Fold glued strip twice with the grain to ¼" x 1½". Use Template: Lilac 1 to cut out the petal shape (d). Open the strip and trim sides to remove bulk (e). Brush a light coat of glue on the bottom half of the petal strip. Wrap it around the stamen, keeping the bottom level so the petal tops are all the same height (it can help to also keep a finger in the center of the bloom as you wrap). Open the strip of petals (f).

6. **To paint the blossoms,** prepare the white gouache with less water than you would normally use. With a fine paintbrush, add a white edge to the petals. If you like, use the remaining dark purple paint to deepen the color of the lower part of the flowers.

Note: Using narrow strips of floral tape to bundle lilac blossoms and buds into clusters before you put them onto the stem helps make the finished stem look tighter and more interesting.

7. **To make bud and blossom clusters,** prepare several narrow strips of floral tape about 5" x ¼" (as on page 24). Cluster blossoms and buds in these combinations or whatever looks appealing to you, keeping in mind that all buds should be at or close to the top.

Two stems: three buds;

One stem: three buds and two blossoms;

Two stems: three buds and three blossoms;

Seven stems: four blossoms.

5. **For the petal strips/sets,** cut against the grain to make nine 2" x 1½" strips of blue mussel crepe (a). Stretch each strip 100% (b). Cut each strip with the grain into four equal parts to make thirty-six small strips. Repeat

8. **To attach flower stems to the main stem,** start with a bud set, and place another bud set about ½" below. Wrap twice with narrow floral tape—just enough to secure. Add a bud-and-blossom set about ½" below. Wrap with tape, making sure buds are close to the stem and blossoms face out. Place one more bud-and-blossom set about ½" below and tape. Nestle the 18-gauge wire into the base of the lilac stem and tape securely. Take a moment to open and reposition the bud-and-blossom stems to your liking. Tape the remaining blossom stem sets in between the gaps, checking that they are about ½" apart as you tape around the stem. Open and reposition blossoms to your liking. Once satisfied, finish floral taping the stem.

Lush Lilac: For a fuller stem, double the number of buds (twenty-four) and blossoms (seventy-two) made with blue mussel crepe. Double the number of 26-gauge wires; cut twenty-four wires into four pieces each to make ninety-six short 4½" stems (twenty-four for buds and seventy-two for blossoms). Consider creating different combinations of buds and blossoms to create a lush statement piece. Consider adding longer stems of emerging flower buds for larger lilac stems to add an extra dimension to your piece. Aim for equal spacing when attaching the buds and blossoms to the stem, leaving about ½ inch of space between each set for a balanced flowering stem.

Chamomile Flower

These dainty blooms add a perfect touch of whimsy to any arrangement, capturing the delicate beauty of chamomile flowers. In this tutorial, I will guide you through crafting these charming flowers, perfect for bunching on a single stem. While I've chosen to omit leaves here to keep the focus on the flowers themselves, feel free to add them separately if you're creating a smaller piece where the greenery could enhance the overall look. The instructions are for making a single flower, but these happy blooms shine when clustered together in a vibrant group.

Additionally, this tutorial offers an exciting opportunity to explore creative projects such as crafting fun floral headwear perfect for special occasions or adding a touch of nature-inspired fashion to your wardrobe. Dive into the project section to find more inspiring ideas on incorporating these lovely chamomile flowers into a monochromatic floral arrangement for your bedside table.

Chamomile Flower

German doublette crepe paper in white/white

German doublette crepe paper in goldenrod/ buttercup

Italian crepe paper in 90 gsm 365 serpentine, for optional leaves

Mod Podge in gloss

one 26-gauge wire

tacky glue

floral tape or Crepe Tape (page 24) in light green (to match serpentine)

Tools: ruler, scissors, scalloped pinking shears (3 mm)

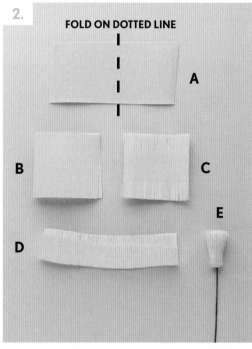

FOLD ON DOTTED LINE

A

B

C

E

D

1. **To prepare the Mod Podge-painted paper,** cut against the grain to make one 3¾" x 1¼" strip of white/white doublette crepe. Paint one side of the strip with gloss Mod Podge. (See Mod Podging, page 23, for more.) Let dry, about one hour.

2. **For the core,** cut against the grain to make one 3½" x 1½" strip goldenrod/buttercup doublette crepe (a). Fold in half with the grain (b). Cut both the top and bottom of the strip in fringe ⅛" x ½" (page 19) (c). Open the strip. Fold the fringed strip lengthwise against the grain, with the lighter yellow facing in and all fringe to one side. Put a thin line of tacky glue down the un-fringed side and fold to glue closed (d). Dot tacky glue along the un-fringed part of the strip. Wrap it around the tip of the 26-gauge wire so the top of the wire hides just below the fringed strip (e). Make sure the stamens are even at the top.

3. To give the stamens a roundish, bulbous shape, make ⅛" angle cuts around them once; then take your time to trim to the shape you like.

4. **For the green stamens,** cut against the grain to make one 2" x 1¾" strip of serpentine. Cut in half with the grain to make two thinner strips (a). Set aside one. Fringe one strip ⅛" x ½" (b). Dot tacky glue along the un-fringed part. Wrap green fringe around the yellow stamens. Trim as needed to even out the green and yellow stamens.

5. **For the sepals,** use scalloped pinking shears to cut across the top of the remaining green strip. With scissors, snip each scallop ¼" deeper (c).

6. **For the petal strips,** accordion fold with the grain the strip of Mod Podge-painted white/white doublette crepe every 1¼" (three times) and cut along the folds to make three smaller strips. Use Template: Chamomile to cut petal shapes into the strips, for a total of three four-petal strips.

4. + 5.

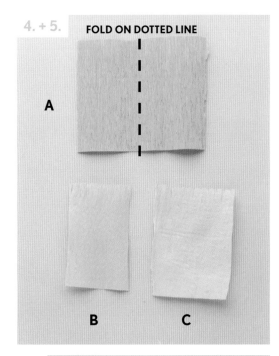

FOLD ON DOTTED LINE

A

B   C

6.

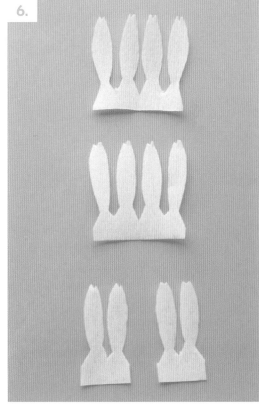

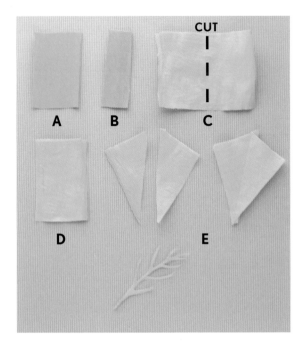

A **B** **CUT** **C**

D **E**

Note: Pinching narrows the base of the petals, so they stand out more.

8. **To attach sepal,** tacky glue it on with the scalloped edges on the petals and peeking between them. Wrap to cover the stem with light green floral tape.

Optional, to add Chamomile Leaves: Cut against the grain to make one 1½" x 2¼" strip of serpentine crepe (a). To laminate the strip, fold it in half with the grain. Brush a thin layer of glue on one inner half. Glue shut (b), and before the glue dries, gently stretch the laminated strip until it is 2½" x 2¼" (c). Let dry. Cut the semi-dry, laminated strip in half with the grain (d). Seam miter (e) as on page 22 with Template: Chamomile Leaf to make one leaf. Put ½" tacky glue down the base. Rub gently to blend it into the stem. Wrap tape to secure the leaf to the main stem about 3" below the flower head.

Note: When placing chamomile leaves, arrange them alternately along the stem. Each leaf appears at a different point, not directly opposite the last. Place them close together for a bushy appearance.

7. **To attach petal strips,** place a line of tacky glue along the base of one four-petal strip. Wrap evenly around the central disc stem, keeping the base high so ⅛" green stamen shows (a). Glue the second four-petal strip to fill in the gaps (b). Make sure the two petal strips are even. Open each petal to face up. Pinch the base of each petal as close as possible to the central disc (this will create more space for the final petal strip, and it will add texture to this beautifully simple flower). Cut the third petal strip in half to make two two-petal strips. Pinch the base of the remaining petals before tacky gluing two-petal strips into the gaps (c).

Night Blooming Cereus or Hoa Quynh

My grandfather passed away many years ago, and I miss him every day. His name is Hoa, which means flowers in Vietnamese. So, not surprisingly, I was also named after a flower, Quynh. My grandfather grew these beautiful flowers in his backyard and would show them off whenever I came by. He reminded me that these were my flowers. In Vietnam, we call it Hoa Quynh. My mother named me after this unique bloom, so this flower will forever hold a special place in my heart.

The night blooming cereus is a large, fragrant flower that blooms on cacti. These rare flowers open at night and close by morning. Some species only flower one night a year! This tutorial creates a stunning white and pink variety, complete with pollen-tipped stamen, delicate pistil, and that unique branching stem that arches off the cactus.

Night Blooming Cereus or Hoa Quynh

German doublette crepe paper in white/white

German doublette crepe paper in leaf/moss

Italian crepe paper in 90 gsm 386 cream

one 16-gauge wire

one 20-gauge wire

tacky glue

floral tape or Crepe Tape (page 24) in white

watercolor or gouache paint in pink and sepia

paintbrushes

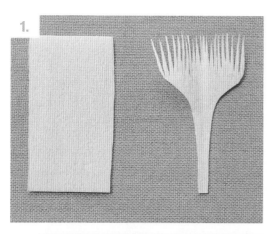

1. **For the pistil,** cut against the grain to make one 1¼" x 2½" strip of white/white doublette crepe. Use Template: Cereus Pistil 1 to cut the bottom part of the pistil. Cut narrow, ⅛" wide x 1" deep darts. Put an even layer of glue on the bottom half.

2. Place the 20-gauge wire right beneath the darts and wrap the pistil around it. Gently open the pistils until flared out evenly around the wire; slightly bend the ends to curve up.

3. **For the stamens,** cut against the grain to make one 6" x 2½" strip of white/white doublette crepe. Accordion fold with the grain every 2" (three times). Cut the folds to make three equal pieces. Cut a ½" x ½" strip of the cream crepe paper and stretch it out 100%. Fold with the grain into thirds. Cut the folds to make three strips. Fold each strip against the grain lengthwise so it is 1½" x ¼".

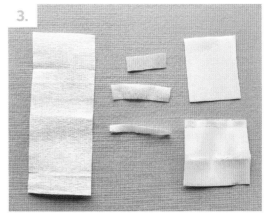

4. Each white/white doublette crepe strip will be glued inside of a cream strip. Let dry before fringing. Follow the instructions for fringing a stamen (page 19).

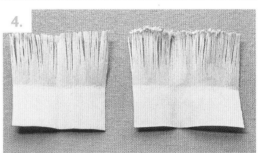

5. Snip off ⅛" from the tops of the fringe until the cream strip is about half the original size. I fold the strip into thirds and then cut. Save the tiny confetti-like pieces for use later.

6. In a small bowl of tacky glue, dip the cream side of the strip lightly into the glue and then dip into the confetti. Make sure each filament has a bit of the confetti glued to the end. Separate the individual filaments so they do not stick together. If they do, just cut them apart after the glue has dried. Complete all three strips and let dry.

7. Cut four large darts at the bottom half of the strips so that there will be less bulk when wrapped around the stem.

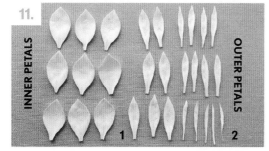

8

INNER PETALS

OUTER PETALS

11.

1

2

12.

8. **For the inner petals,** cut one 25" x 2½" strip of white/white doublette crepe. Accordion fold with the grain every 2¾" (nine times). Cut the folds to create nine pieces. Fold the strips in half, with the grain. Spread a thin layer of glue evenly across one-half and glue each shut; with the glue still damp, use Template: Cereus 1 to cut out nine inner petals. Before glue dries, cup and shape (see Cupping, page 17).

9. **For the outer petals 1,** cut one 10½" x 2½" strip white/white doublette crepe. Accordion fold with the grain every 1½" (seven times). Cut the folds to create seven pieces. Fold each strip in half with the grain, spread glue stick on one inner half, and shut. Before the glue dries, use Template: Cereus 2 to cut seven outer petals.

10. Curl tips around an awl, then cup and shape them.

11. **For the outer petals 2,** cut one 15" x 2½" strip of white/white doublette crepe. Accordion fold with the grain every 1½" (ten times). Cut the folds to make ten strips. To laminate them, fold each one in half with the grain, spread glue stick on one inner half and shut; before the glue dries, use Template: Cereus 3 to cut the laminated strips into ten outer petals. Curl the tip of the petal around an awl, then cup and shape before it dries. Cut one of these petals in half. Cut another petal into three slimmer pieces, for a total of thirteen. Let dry.

12. **To paint,** wet a paintbrush and mix to combine pink and sepia watercolors in varying shades of light and dark pink. Use them to paint both sides of all thirteen outer petals 2.

13. **To assemble the center:** Glue stamens to pistil wire by making a big U around the main stem with fringe, working in layers:

> **Layer 1:** Center a stamen strip in the middle of the pistil wire. Carefully gather the darts and glue around the stamen.

> **Layer 2:** With the next stamen strip, place glue on each of the darts. Fold in half to glue shut. Slightly cup where the darts and the filaments meet. Place another line of glue on the two remaining darts and place on the right side of the pistil wire.

> **Layer 3:** Repeat the Layer 2 instructions with the final strip, but glue on the left side.

Carefully reach inside and shape the stamens into a U-shape. Leave a slight gap at the top. Curve the stamens slightly inward toward the pistil.

14. **To attach the inner petals:**

> **Layer 1:** Glue three petals in a triangular pattern on the top of the U, then lower left and lower right.

> **Layer 2:** Add three petals between the gaps formed by the first layer.

> **Layer 3:** Add three petals between the gaps formed by the second layer.

15.

16.

15. To attach the outer petals: Glue outer petals 1 in between the gaps until all are used. Glue outer petals 2 in between the gaps.

16. To attach the slim petals: These five slimmer petals will be the final layer. These petals should curve away from the bloom a bit, with the tips arching upward. Use white floral tape on the bottom of the petals.

17. To finish the foliage and stem: Wrap white floral tape about 2½" to 3" down from the petals. Wrap tape to thicken this layer to about ¼". With pointed scissors, cut tiny snips into the stem, creating spines. To paint, ready a cup of water to wet and clean your brush. Mix pink and sepia to make a dark pink color. Paint the stem and base. Let dry.

Tip: if the stamens are glued together, instead of pulling them apart with your fingers, use your scissors to cut them apart. If you do not see the gap easily, turn the flower over and the gaps will become more visible.

18. For the stem, place stem next to 16-gauge wire, the tops of both about even. Bend cereus stem about 3" down. Firmly tape the wires together at the bend and work downward. The end of the 16-gauge wire will be poking up a few inches (a). Cut one 5" x 10" strip from the leaf/moss doublette crepe. Fold strip in half with the grain with the darker moss green on the inside, so the fold is now 2½" wide. Use Template: Cereus Stem to cut out the stem (b). Spread an even coat of glue over the inside of the stem pieces (c). Place the 16-gauge wire down the middle of the stem and glue shut (d). Let dry.

17.

18a.

18b.

18c.

18d.

Night Blooming Cereus or Hoa Quynh

Spray Rose:
Princess Fairy Kiss

Spray roses are dainty beauties with several smaller blooms and buds (or "sprays") per stem. Due to their small size, paper spray roses' delicate blooms require precise engineering to ensure they are dainty and yet robust enough to resist aging over time. One of the most effective techniques for strengthening crepe paper is lamination with glue.

This tutorial takes you on a step-by-step instruction to recreate every blooming stage of a spray garden rose's life. You will start with the tight bud and progress to the full splendor of bloom. The tutorial guides you on the petal placement needed to create one fully bloomed rose and a stem of five leaves. At any point, you can pause to add the calyx, capturing the rose in different stages of growth. This allows you to assemble a varied and visually captivating cluster of spray roses.

You will learn to shape the young buds, which are more closed and compact, and to gradually open the petals as you progress to the later stages of bloom. Paying close attention to the calyx at the base of each bud and bloom is crucial; this green, leaf-like structure supports the petals and enhances the realism of your paper roses. By incorporating all these stages, your finished arrangement will present a stunningly beautiful cluster of spray garden roses in various phases of their life cycle, providing depth and intrigue to your floral creations.

Spray Rose: Princess Fairy Kiss

German doublette crepe paper in light rose/pink

Italian crepe paper in 90 gsm rosa 384

Italian crepe paper in 90 gsm serpentine 365

five 6" 26-gauge wires

one 22-gauge wire, for the main stem

one ¾" spun cotton ball

tacky glue

glue stick

floral tape or Crepe Tape (page 24) in medium green

Tools: ruler, scissors, wire cutter, paintbrushes, awl

1. – 3.

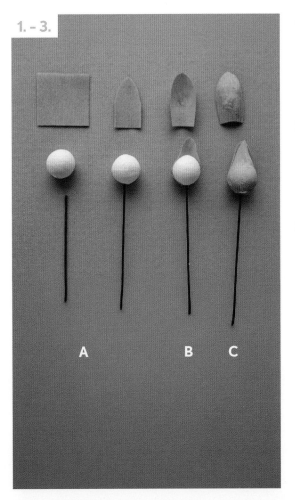

A   B   C

1. **For the core,** dot tacky glue at the hole on the spun cotton ball. Attach wire by sticking one end into the glue-lined hole, make sure the glue gets on the top of the wire as you insert it (a).

2. Cut one 1½" square of light rose/pink doublette crepe paper. Fold in half with the grain. Use Template: Spray Rose Bud 1 to cut out two bud-shaped pieces. Deep cup each piece (b).

3. Brush an even layer of glue on the bottom two-thirds of each piece and arrange them opposite each other on the spun cotton ball. Mold the pieces around the spun cotton, closing over the top (c).

Tip: When laminating spray rose petals, it is important to swiftly shape them into their natural curved form before the glue sets, so they will have a soft, lifelike appearance.

4. **For the bud petals,** avoid stretching the crepe and cut against the grain to make one 10" x 2" strip of 90 gsm rosa (a). Accordion fold with the grain every 2" (five times) (b). Cut the folds to make five pieces. To laminate them, spread a thin layer of glue stick on one side of each piece and fold over lengthwise (c); before the glue dries, use Template: Spray Rose 1 to cut five petals (d). Open each one carefully; the paper will be fragile with wet glue. Gently cup each petal (e). Brush an even layer of glue to the bottom two-thirds of two of these cupped petals; place them opposite each other on the bud's center (f). They should cover the first layer, sitting about ⅛" higher. Use an awl to curl the right top of the remaining three petals (g). Brush on some glue to the bottom two-thirds of all three.

5. **To attach the bud petals** evenly around the center, place one curled petal over a seam on the spun cotton ball. Its cupped base should hug the ball while the tip curls outward. Add the next curled petal, covering the non-curled half of the last. Add the final petal, again covering half of the last and tucking in the other side so all three curled petals sit snugly and evenly around the bud's center. To complete the bud, you'll add calyxes now. To make a blooming rose, continue on with the following steps.

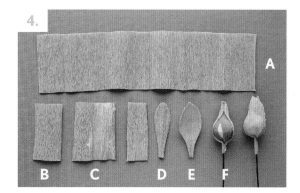

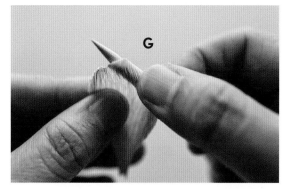

7.

9.

TOP VIEW

SIDE VIEW

THE NEW ART OF PAPER FLOWERS

6. **For the opening bloom's petals,** avoid stretching the crepe and cut against the grain to make one 6" x 2" strip of rosa. Accordion fold with the grain every 1" (six times). Cut the folds to create six pieces. Use Template: Spray Rose 1 to cut six petals.

7. To shape, deeply cup each petal. Use an awl to curl the right side and a bit of the middle edge of each one.

8. **To attach to the flower head:** Dot the base of each petal with glue and arrange all six shaped petals around the flower head. Layer some edges as you did for the bud, but keep most edges more open.

9. **For the mostly bloomed petals,** avoid stretching the crepe and cut against the grain to make one 12" x 2" strip of rosa crepe. Accordion fold with the grain every 1" (twelve times). Cut the folds to make twelve pieces. Use Template: Spray Rose 1 to cut those pieces into twelve petals.

10. **To shape,** deeply cup each one. Curl the right and left edge of each petal with an awl.

11. Deepen each cupped and curled petal's bloom with mitering as on page 22. Cut ½" slit into the center of each mitered petal's base. Put a dot of tacky glue on the right side of the slit and cross the left over to form an X. Repeat with each petal.

10.

11.

13.

15.

16.

A   B   C   D   E

12. **To attach to the flower head:** Dot glue all twelve deeply bloomed petals between the gaps of the opening blooms of the earlier layer on the flower head.

13. **For the fully bloomed petals,** avoid stretching the crepe and cut one 12½" x 2" strip of rosa crepe. Accordion fold with the grain every 1¼" (ten times). Cut the folds to make ten pieces. Use Template: Spray Rose 2 to cut them into petals.

14. **To shape,** deeply cup each petal. Deeply curl the right and left edges with an awl to create an almost V-shaped petal edge. Bloom them even more with overlap mitering as on page 23. Cut a ¼" slit at the base. Place a dot of glue on the right side of the slit and cross the left over to form an X. Repeat with each petal.

15. **To attach to the flower head:** Glue the petals between the gaps of the last layer on the rose's head, working in two rows of five petals each.

   Note: Make sure these deeply bloomed petals nest tightly close to the center of the flower head. (Do not glue them onto the wire stem, or you will have a sagging bloom.)

16. **For the calyxes,** cut with the grain to make one 5" x 3" strip of serpentine. Accordion fold with the grain every 1" (five times). Cut the folds to make five pieces (a). Spread a thin layer of glue on the side of each one; fold in half with the grain (b) and, before glue dries, use Template: Spray Rose Calyx 1 to cut five calyxes (c). Gently open each calyx shape, remembering the wet paper is fragile, and slightly cup each one (d). Cut slim (½" to ¾") darts on both sides of each calyx (e).

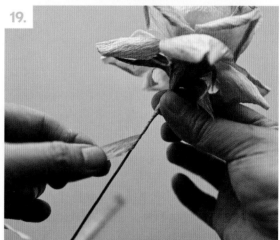

17. **To attach to the flower head:** Glue the five shaped calyxes, equally spaced, around the base of the flower head. Cut about 7" x ¼" strip of green crepe to use as tape. Tacky glue it around the base of the calyxes. Continue wrapping down to tape the stem.

Note: This rose leaf has a smoother edge, less saw-toothed than other species.

18. **For the leaves:** Cut against the grain to make one 9¾" x 3" strip of serpentine. Accordion fold with the grain every 1⅝" (six times). Cut the folds to make six pieces. Use Template: Rose Leaf to cut six leaves (you only need five for one spray rose and can save the remaining leaf for later use). Shape and wire them by seam mitering (as on page 22) with five 6" 26-gauge wires that stick out halfway for 3" stems.

19. **To finish the leaves and stem,** cut a strip of green crepe to use as floral tape, about 7" x ¼". Wrap tape down 1¾" from the flower head and attach a pair of leaves opposite each other. Tape down another 1¾", secure another a pair of leaves opposite each other, and wrap tape to the end of the stem wire.

20. **For a full spray of roses:** Repeat steps to make three to five more roses—enough to make a cluster for one spray rose stem. Leave space between each rose head so they are not too crowded. I like to wrap tape down the stem about 2" to 4" before adding another bloom. Tape down 1¾" and attach a pair of leaves if desired.

Note: If you are making spray roses for an arrangement or bouquet, omit the leaves or make them as a stand-alone stem so you can more freely arrange them. In larger arrangements, individual foliage stems are a framework or armature for holding arranged blossoms in place.

Poppy: Amazing Gray

Creating the center of this poppy was a delightful challenge! Sometimes, we must think creatively and use unconventional materials to achieve the desired results. For this project, I turn to a lightweight and versatile modeling clay to sculpt the poppy's detailed pollen-dusted stamens and pistil. Layers of soft pastels add deep, vibrant, complex color to the pistil, oval-shaped anthers, and dark filaments of the stamen, and they give a two-tone inner and outer petal of poppy. The "Amazing Gray" variety inspired this poppy tutorial, which guides you through each step of constructing a lifelike poppy as well as techniques for applying layers of shadowy color with an amazing effect. But I encourage you to experiment with any coloring mediums and colors you like. Whether you choose watercolors, acrylics, or even markers, each medium brings a unique look to your creation. Take the artistic freedom to personalize your flowers, making each one uniquely yours.

Poppy: Amazing Gray

Italian crepe paper in 90 gsm 378 lilla chiaro

German doublette crepe paper in white/white

spun cotton ball (15 mm)

one 20-gauge wire, for main stem

tacky glue

UV archival spray

floral tape or Crepe Tape (page 24) in medium
green

modeling clay, such as Crayola Model Magic,
in white

soft pastels in lime, dark green, and purple,
such as PanPastels in 680.3 bright
yellow-green shade, 660.1 chrome ox
green extra dark, and 470.5 violet

Tools: ruler, scissors, awl, makeup brushes
(preferably one for each color) for
applying soft pastels

110

2. – 4.

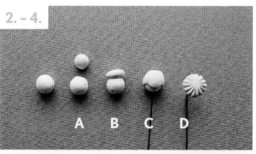

5.

1. **For the pistil,** dot tacky glue onto the hole
   in the spun cotton ball. Push one end of the
   20-gauge wire into the hole through the glue.
   Let dry.

2. Take a small, marble-size pinch of modeling
   clay and roll it into a ball (a). Place a dot of tacky
   glue on top of the hole in the spun cotton ball.
   Gently press the modeling clay ball on top of the
   glue. Flip it over and flatten the modeling clay by
   pressing it on a flat surface (b).

3. Turn it back over and, keeping the clay about ⅛"
   thick, carefully press down until the spun cotton
   ball until is two-thirds covered (c).

4. Using the point of an awl, carve a line starting ⅛"
   from the center down the side. Make a similar
   line on the opposite side. Carve two more lines
   to form a plus sign. Between each line, make two
   more lines, for a total of twelve equally spaced
   indented lines (d).

5. **To add color:** Use a separate makeup brush for each color, if you can, and brush or rub so there is no loose powder remaining in between layers.

> **Layer 1:** Cover the surface with a layer of yellow-green soft pastel.

> **Layer 2:** Brush on the dark (ox) green, starting in the center of the pistil, and then into the twelve indented lines.

> **Layer 3:** Color the dark green lines with violet. Spray the finished piece with UV archival spray to set the color. Let dry several hours or overnight.

6. – 8.

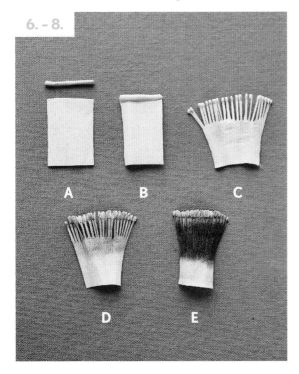

6. **For the stamens,** cut against the grain to make four 1" x 1½" strips of white/white doublette crepe.

Note: If you are having a hard time putting the clay cylinders onto crepe strips, run your awl down each cylinder in an even line. Fill that line with a fine line of tacky glue. Place each glue-lined cylinder onto the edge of its crepe strip, and gently press the sides down into the paper.

7. Roll four small pieces of modeling clay into four slender cylinders about ⅛" wide x 1" long (a). Carefully place a cylinder along the top edge of each paper strip (b). Gently press the sides and top down while keeping the cylinder shape of the clay. Clean clay edges as needed by running the point of your awl along them in a straight line. Let dry for 10 to 15 minutes, or until the clay is not tacky to the touch. Working quickly as the clay dries fast, cut to fringe each strip of white/white doublette crepe (as on page 19), about ⅛" wide and ¾" deep (c). Before the glue dries, stretch the fringed strips 30% to separate the filaments and keep the modeling clay from sticking to itself. Using the point of an awl, press gently but firmly on the sides of each clay filament to make an imprint. This will flatten to make your unique pollen tip. If needed, use your scissors to cut the clay pollen again so they do not stick together.

8. **To add color,** use a flat brush to apply the first layer of yellow-green pastel on the top two-thirds (d). Use a different flat brush to apply the second layer of soft pastel color in violet, coloring only the filament and leaving the pollen tip yellow green (e). Coat with UV spray to set the layers of soft pastel. Let dry.

9. **For the inner petals,** cut against the grain to make one 12" x 2" strip of lilla chiaro. Accordion fold with the grain every 1" (twelve times) and cut the folds to make twelve pieces. Use Template: Poppy 1 to cut them into petals.

10. **To color,** apply soft pastel in violet at the base of each petal, and then brush up, leaving the top third uncolored. Brush color along the edge of the top third to outline each petal. Coat with UV archival spray to set the soft pastel color. Let dry.

11. **For the outer petals,** cut one 9" x 2½" strip of lilla chiaro crepe. Accordion fold with the grain every 2¼" (4 times) to make four pieces. Use Template: Poppy 2 to cut them into four petals.

12. Use a makeup brush to apply violet pastel at the top of each petal and brush it down to the base.

13. Add a few lines of tacky glue from the middle of each petal to the base. Avoid stretching the crepe; with your thumb, rub the glue evenly across each petal. Gather each base in tiny pleats and twist. (It's okay if you have pleats in the upper part of a petal, it will be stretched out after the petal is dried.) Let dry.

14. **To shape,** gently stretch the top part of each petal (a). Add ruffles about every ½" along each petal edge (b). (See page 24 for more on Ruffling.)

15. **To assemble the center,** tacky glue the four stamen strips evenly around the pistil. Make sure the carved lines of pollen face out, and the pollen tips float about ½" above the pistil (not too high). The stamens should look like eyelashes surrounding an eye. Take a moment to curve them in; this will help create movement in this lovely flower.

   Note: I like to make sure each petal has some air between it and the next petal. By giving them some air, you will make each petal stand out on its own.

16. **To attach the petals to the flower head:** Ruffle all twelve inner petals, and then tacky glue them on in layers.

   Layer 1: Add about seven petals in a row around the center.

   Layer 2: Add about five petals, placed to fill in the gaps.

   Layer 3: Add two outer petals opposite each other.

   Layer 4: Place the remaining two outer petals in the gaps.

17. **To finish:** Pull each petal down and out to open the flower. You may want to re-ruffle the petals as well. Wrap with tape from under the flower head to the end of the stem.

Icelandic Poppy

LEVEL: 7

This tutorial is designed to guide you through the process of thickening a stem while keeping it flexible enough to create the playful, wonky movements characteristic of these vibrant, colorful poppies. When selecting paper, opt for a lightweight yet resilient type to stretch and re-crepe effectively. I highly recommend using German extra fine crepe paper or Italian 90 gsm crepe paper for best results. These materials provide the durability needed for manipulation and the delicacy needed for a natural papery appearance. Consider creating a unified color scheme by mixing a large diluted watercolor base paint and then dipping several complementary colors into it. This technique ensures that all the elements of your arrangement share a harmonious underlying tone, enhancing the overall aesthetic cohesion of your floral display.

Icelandic Poppy

SUPPLIES

Italian crepe paper in 90 gsm 360 rose distant drum

German doublette crepe paper in white/white

German doublette crepe paper in goldenrod/buttercup

watercolor or gouache paint, in dark pink (or red plus white)

one 20-gauge wire

clear plastic tube (³⁄₁₆")

tacky glue

floral tape or Crepe Tape (page 24) in medium green

alcohol marker, such as Copic, in lime-yellow

soft pastel in lime, such as PanPastel in 680.3 bright yellow-green shade

spun cotton ball (15 mm)

modeling clay, such as Crayola Model Magic, in white

UV archival spray

Tools: ruler, scissors, paintbrushes, wire cutter

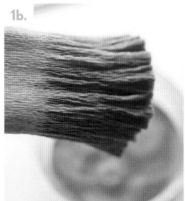

Tip: Try soaking crepe in watercolor-tinted water for a beautiful effect. If you soak extra fine crepe, be incredibly careful when moving it; it tends to tear much easier than 90 gsm.

1. **To prepare the painted paper:** Cut against the grain to make one 26" x 3" strip of distant drum rose crepe. Use a brush to mix dark pink watercolor paint into a cup of water. Roll the strip and dip one end into the paint (a). Let the color soak about one-third up the paper. Once you are satisfied with the color absorption, pull it out and turn it upside-down to let the paint run down (b). Let it air dry or use a hair dryer to speed up the process. Cut the dry strip into four 5" strips and three 2" strips. Use Template: Icelandic Poppy 1 to cut four petals from the 5" strips. Use Template: Icelandic Poppy 2 to cut three petals from the 2" strips.

2c.

2d.

2. **To shape,** tightly twist all seven petals with the grain. Gently unroll them. Add thin lines of tacky glue on the bottom one-third of one textured petal. Rub it into the crepe with your thumb (a). Make small, ¼" to ⅛" pleats along the edge of a textured petal (b). Let dry. Repeat to pleat all remaining six petals. Once pleated petals are dry, gently stretch out the tops (c). Ruffle about every ½" or so along each top. With an awl, curl some parts of the petal edges toward you and some away from you (d). This will help create movement.

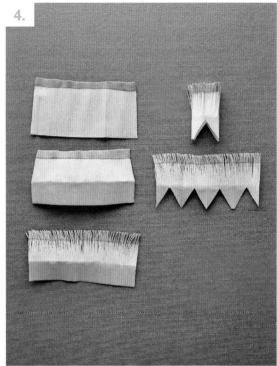

3. **For the pistil,** follow the poppy pistil instructions on page 110, stopping when you reach the coloring stage. Color the twelve lines with lime-yellow alcohol marker. Apply a second layer of color with yellow-green pastel, covering the entire pistil except the lime-yellow lines. Coat the finished pistil with UV archival spray to set the soft pastel colors. (See page 24 for more.)

4. **For the stamen,** cut against the grain to make three 3½" x 1" strips of goldenrod/buttercup doublette crepe. Fold each strip in half against the grain, the lighter yellow (goldenrod) facing in. Cut three 3½" x 2" white/white strips of doublette crepe. Follow the instructions for Fringing to Make a Stamen (page 19), cutting as narrowly as possible, at most 1/16" wide. Cut darts along the white edge of the strip to lessen the bulk.

5. **To assemble the flower center,** glue the three stamen strips evenly around the pistil.

6. **To attach petals to the flower head:** Tacky glue the three smaller petals evenly around the center. Make sure the tips of the petals are all level to each other. Take one larger petal and glue it behind the biggest gap in the first row. The next petal should go behind the next large gap. Turn the flower head over and place the last petals in the last two gaps, making sure the flower is balanced. Take your time to add ruffles and curl your petals, some backward and some curling toward you. Use your awl to create tighter curls and your fingers to create looser curls. Do not be afraid to exaggerate the curls.

7. **To finish the stem:** Floral tape about 1" from the base of the flower head. Place a thin line of glue around the base of the flower head. Slide the plastic tube over the wire and glue in place. Floral tape your stem to cover the entire plastic tube. Bend and shape how you want your stem to look, and you are done!

5.

6.

Single Peony: Claire de Lune

The Claire de Lune is an early summer flowering single peony with impressive seven-inch flowers. At first bloom, the petals are a soft yellow reminiscent of the glow of moonlight. Over time, the color shifts to a creamy ivory. This ephemeral color transition adds a layer of intrigue to this beautifully understated peony. I use white/white doublette crepe paper to make an older Claire de Lune with white petals that show off the lush yellow stamens at the center of the flower. Consider a white/ivory doublette crepe to make a just-bloomed flower. This tutorial will show you how to make bulbous carpels and their lush stamens and where to place the petals around this peony's center to create an elegant bloom. Most of your time will be spent crafting and fringing the stamens. After painting your crepe paper with Mod Podge, use the drying time efficiently by preparing your stamens. This step ensures you can seamlessly continue your project once the crepe paper is ready.

Single Peony: Claire de Lune

German doublette crepe paper in white/white

Italian crepe paper in 90 gsm 352 ivory

German doublette crepe paper in leaf/moss for leaves

Italian crepe paper in 90 gsm 366 olive

German doublette crepe paper in goldenrod/ buttercup

German doublette crepe paper in white/ivory

seven 26-gauge wires, cut in half to make fourteen 9" pieces

one 18-gauge paper-covered wire, for main stem

tacky glue

Mod Podge in matte and gloss

floral tape in medium green or Crepe Tape (page 24) in leaf/moss

Tools: ruler, scissors, wire cutter, and paintbrushes

Note: For more on technique and to prepare and store entire sheets of crepe paper for later use, see Large-Batch Mod Podging (page 23).

1. **To prepare matte and gloss Mod Podge-painted crepe:** Cut against the grain to make one 40" x 3" strip white/white doublette crepe. Use a wide, flat brush to paint one side with matte Mod Podge. Cut against the grain to make one 12" x 3" strip and one 1" x 2" strip of leaf/moss doublette crepe. Paint the lighter (leaf-colored) sides with gloss Mod Podge. Let dry, 1 to 3 hours.

Note: Most peonies have a slight sheen. I like to use gloss Mod Podge to put a similar sheen on crepe paper. It adds durability, too, helping flowers keep their form and elegance. This is particularly good for flowers that have a substantial number of stamens and only a single layer of petals.

2. **For the stigmas,** cut with the grain to make one 1½" x 1" strip ivory crepe. Accordion fold with the grain every ⅜" (four times). Cut the folds to make four slim strips (a). Put a thin line of tacky glue along the bottom two-thirds of each one. Place one 9" 26-gauge wire on top of each glue-lined center, leaving the top third open and unwired for the exposed stigma (b). Fold strips in half over the wires. Fan the ends to give each stigma a slight flare.

Note: The number of crepe paper strips you use for your carpels depends on how thick or thin you want them to be and how you wrap. If you wrap loosely, you will use less; if you wrap tightly, you will use more of the paper.

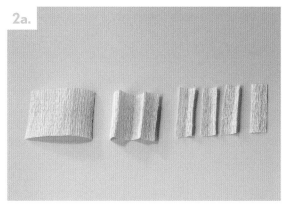

2a.

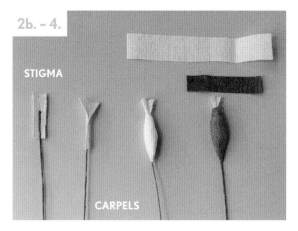

2b. – 4.

STIGMA

CARPELS

5.

3. **For the carpels,** cut against the grain to make one 12" x ¼" strip white/white doublette crepe. Accordion fold every 3" (four times). Cut the folds to make four strips. Slightly stretch the crepe to lengthen each strip from 3" to 5". Put thin lines of tacky glue on the strips. Start wrapping a glue-lined strip just below a flared stigma. Work down about an inch, then crisscross back up. Bulk up the middle of the carpel and taper at either end. Use more strips as needed. Repeat on all four stigma wires.

4. Cut against the grain to make four 1½" x ¼" strips of olive crepe. Stretch 100%. Use it to tightly cover the carpels, keeping the stigmas exposed. Before the glue dries, mold each carpel into a concave shape with the back of your scissors or an awl.

5. Hold the carpels together in a diamond shape. Insert the 18-gauge wire in the center of the carpel set. Place a large glue dot in the center and press firmly so the stem and carpels are secure. Tape the carpel stem with 5" floral tape. Let dry about fifteen minutes.

6. **For the stamens,** laminate and fringe (as on page 19) eight 6" x 2" strips of white/ivory doublette crepe and eight 6" x 1" strips of goldenrod/buttercup doublette crepe. Apply a thin line of tacky glue along the bottom of one fringed stamen strip. Stack a second stamen strip on top and press or use binder clips to hold the layers together, making sure the yellow tops stay even. Repeat three more times to make a total of four laminated strips of stamens.

Note: Do you need a shortcut? Instead of cutting, stretching, and gluing strips of olive crepe over the carpels to make them green, you can quickly color them with soft pastels or another coloring medium.

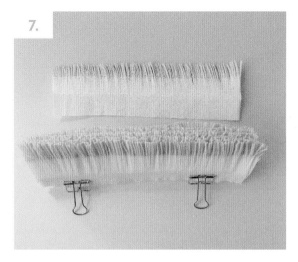

7.

7a.

7b.

7. **To assemble the center,** apply a line of tacky glue to the bottom of one laminated strip of stamens. Place the carpel stem at one end so that the carpels sit centered within the white part (a). The pollen will sit above the flared stigma about ½". Wrap the stamen strip tightly around the flared stigma (b). Press firmly into place to bloom open the stamens.

8. **For the petals,** use the Mod Podge-painted white/white doublette crepe to cut against the grain to make 1 Petals Strip: 16" x 2", accordion fold every 1¾" and cut the folds to make nine pieces. Use Template: Claire de Lune Petal to cut nine petals. For the guard petals, use the Mod Podge-painted white/white doublette crepe to cut against the grain to make one guard petal strip: 14" x 3", accordion fold every 2", and cut the folds to make seven pieces. Use Template: Claire de Lune Guard Petal to cut seven petals.

9. **To shape,** cup and ruffle the nine petals (see Ruffling, page 24). (You can also cut tiny, smooth waves along the petal tops, then curl them under to create ripples.)

10. Slightly cup the seven guard petals for a round, smooth look (these are not as deeply cupped as the nine petals).

11. **To finish the flower head,** add one dot of tacky glue to the base of each petal and guard petal. Attach them evenly around the center in batches.

> **Row 1:** Start with two petals. Attach them like bunny ears, pressing the glued ends firmly to the top of the core right next to the assembled center. Place three more petals around the center, not too evenly.

> **Row 2:** Add four petals, placing them to cover the gaps between the first layer petals, and varying placement to create interest.

> **Row 3:** Dot tacky glue onto the bases of the seven guard petals and place them on one at a time. As you work, flip the flower head over occasionally to look for any gaps.

12. **For the leaves,** overlap miter as on page 23, using one 12" x 3" strip Mod Podge-painted leaf/moss crepe cut into eight 1½" strips; miter six leaves with Template: Peony Leaf A and one leaf with Template: Peony Leaf B. Place four 9" wire stems in three of Template: Leaf A and one in the Template: Leaf B. Set aside the three unwired mitered leaves to use as bracts later. (You'll have enough paper for one extra leaf you can use on a later project.)

13.

13. To make a leaf set, arrange the four wired and mitered glossy leaves. Start with Leaf B in the middle, add one Leaf A to the right. Add another Leaf A slightly below it. Wrap with floral tape. Continue wrapping tape down the wire about 2". Place the last Leaf A. Continue taping until no wires are exposed.

Note: Sepals hold up your flower head and hide any parts that you do not want to be seen.

14. For the sepals, from the 1" x 2" Mod Podge-painted leaf/moss doublette crepe, cut three Template: Sepals A and three Template: Sepals B. With the painted side facing out, cup the top third of each sepal until slightly concave.

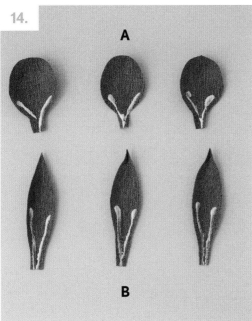

14.

15. **To finish the flower head,** draw a V of tacky glue on the bottom half of each sepal. Glue sepals over gaps at flower base as follows.

> **Layer 1:** Attach Sepals A in a triangle pattern around the flower base.

> **Layer 2:** Attach Sepals B between gaps of the sepals attached first.

16. **To finish the foliage and stem,** tape to put the first bract slightly below the base of the sepals on the underside of the flower head. Continue taping down about 1" and add the second bract. Add the third and final bract slightly offset from the second bract. Tape down about 2½" and tape to secure the finished leaf set. Check the view from the top to be sure the leaves are visible before taping securely to the stem. To finish, wrap tape down the rest of the stem.

15.

Semi-Double Peony: Coral Charm

LEVEL: 7

The Coral Charm is a semi-double peony that captivates with its remarkable color transformation, beginning as a deep persimmon before gradually shifting through shades of coral to a final cream hue as its petals prepare to fall. This tutorial is designed to guide you in creating a vibrant coral peony, using carefully selected shades of crepe paper to mimic the natural color progression. I have included detailed steps for crafting a bright coral bloom and notes on adjusting the tones for a softer, more subdued flower. Feel free to experiment with different shades of crepe to capture the stunning variety of peonies at various stages of their bloom. Additionally, get creative with the dyeing process—consider using leftover scrap colors or even watercolors to add a unique touch to your petals. Try these different techniques to achieve unique results that make each bloom distinctively yours. I cannot wait to see you make these fun Coral Charm peonies. Make sure to tag me @pinkandposey on Instagram so I can see your beautiful work!

Semi-Double Peony: Coral Charm

German doublette crepe paper in leaf/moss

scraps of German doublette crepe paper in red/wine, 3" x 3" or bigger for a more concentrated petal dye

seven scraps crepe paper in light colors, at least 3½" x ¼" each

German doublette crepe paper in light pink/rose

German doublette crepe paper in white/white

German doublette crepe paper in goldenrod/buttercup

Italian crepe paper in 90 gsm 366 green olive

three 26-gauge wires, cut into thirds for nine 6" stems (set aside two of them, as this tutorial uses only seven 6" stems)

seven 28-gauge wires in white, cut into thirds to make twenty-one 6" stems

one 18-gauge wire, for main stem

Mod Podge in gloss

tacky glue

floral tape or Crepe Tape (page 24) made with Italian crepe paper in 90 gsm 366 green olive

UV-resistant clear coating

Tools: scissors, wire cutters, paintbrushes, awl

Note: I highly recommend doing a sample dye test on a scrap before dying all the crepe.

1. **For the shiny leaf paper:** Cut with the grain to make one 4" x 12" strip of leaf/moss doublette crepe. Paint the lighter (leaf-colored) side of the strip with gloss Mod Podge. Let dry, 1 to 3 hours.

2. **For the dip-dyed petal paper:** Ready a cup or other short container of room temperature water and put on gloves. Put a 3" x 3" (or larger) scrap of red/wine doublette crepe into the water. The color will bleed into the water. Take the paper out once you are happy with the color, usually about a minute or so. Add more scraps or watercolor to deepen the color.

3. **To dip-dye,** without unfolding, cut two 3" tall strips of the red/wine crepe. (The best method is to use a guillotine cutter and cut 3" off one end.) Put one end of a fold into the water. Let it soak halfway up, about 10 to 15 seconds, and then take it out of the water. Stand it upright with the dyed end up so that the color runs down and creates an ombre dye. Dip and stand again until you achieve the color you want. Repeat with the other strip. Let dry 100% before unfolding.

4. If you want to add another layer of color, you can re-dye dry crepe with the remaining dyed water. Try using a paintbrush to color specific parts instead of coloring the whole piece again.

Note: Do not unfold the watercolor-painted strips of crepe while they are drying in step 3. Keeping these delicate pieces folded protects them against tearing.

5. **For the stigmas,** cut with the grain to make one 1¾" x 1" strip of light pink/rose doublette crepe. Accordion fold with the grain every ¼" (seven times). Cut the folds to make seven strips. Put thin lines of tacky glue on the bottom two-thirds of each one. Place one 6" wire onto the tacky glue in the center of each one, leaving the top third open and unwired for an exposed stigma. Wrap the paper around the wires. Fan the end to give the stigma a slight flare. Let dry.

6. **For the carpel,** cut against the grain to make one 3½" x ¼" scrap of light-colored crepe. Stretch out strips 100%. To bulk up the wires, tacky glue stretched strips around the wire starting at the base of the stigma and working up, but do not tape the top fourth where the stigma is flared. To build more bulk in the middle, continue taping up and down on the diagonal, crossing at the center, until you are happy with the size.

7. **To finish the carpels,** cut against the grain to make several 4" x ½" strips of green olive crepe to into crepe tape; stretch strips 100% and use with tacky glue to cover the seven carpels (but not the flared stigma). Before the glue has dried, mold the carpels into a concave shape with your fingers or awl.

8. Arrange the molded carpels into a circle. Once you are happy with their placement, insert the (uncut) 18-gauge wire into the center of the circle. Place a large dot of tacky glue in the center and press firmly to secure the wire. Tape around the base of the carpels to hold. Let dry.

6. + 7.

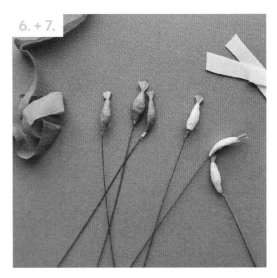

8.

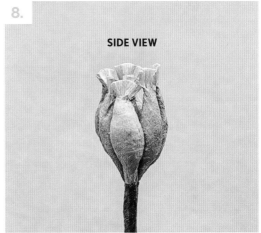

SIDE VIEW

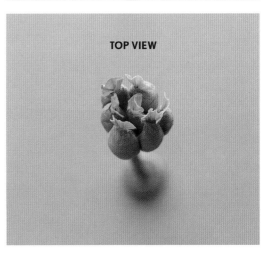

TOP VIEW

9. **For the stamens,** laminate and fringe as on page 19, folding eight 4" x 1" strips of goldenrod/buttercup doublette crepe each in half with the darker yellow (buttercup) side facing out, and using a glue stick to laminate in pairs of two with eight 4" x 2" strips of white/white doublette crepe. Fringe with cuts 1/16" apart and 1" into the yellow edge of each laminated strip to make eight fringed strips of stamens. Put a line of tacky glue at the bottom of one fringed strip and place another strip on top; check that the yellow tops line up (a). Repeat, layering three more sets of fringed stamen strips to make a total of four thick fringed stamen strips.

10. **To shape,** bend the yellow pieces of fringe over your thumb and press (b). Slightly stretch out the paper at the base of the stamens (c). Glue one shaped fringe around the base of the carpel stem, keeping the top even. Wrap and glue all four stamen strips (d). Press the base firmly to the stem to open the center and show the carpels (e).

9.

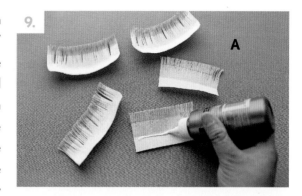

A

10b.

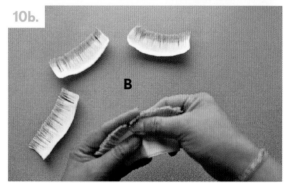

B

10c.

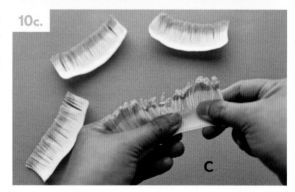

C

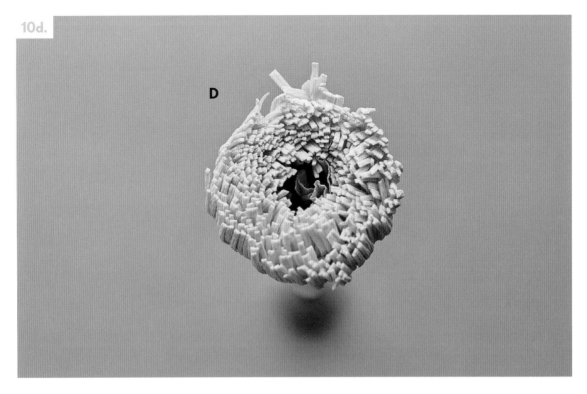

D

E

11. **For the wired petals,** cut the remaining 28-gauge wires into thirds to make twenty-one pieces. Unfold the dry strip of dyed crepe. Accordion fold with the grain every 2" (sixteen times). Cut the folds to make sixteen pieces and set one aside for a future project; here you will use fifteen. Cut the stack from point to point to create thirty triangles (a). Overlap miter them into petals as on page 23, wiring each with one with a 6" piece of 28-gauge wire about ½" below the top (b).

12. **To shape,** trim to round the top three corners of each kite-shaped petal (c). Slightly cup all fifteen rounded, wired petals, focusing on the center and edges (d). Wrap petal edges around an awl to curl them toward you. Lightly ruffle the edges. Bend the wires so each petal lays open (e).

13. **For the guard petals,** with the rest of the dyed strip, accordion fold with the grain every 3" (five times). Cut the folds to make five strips. Overlap miter to make five guard petals, placing one 28-gauge wire 1" below each top and rounding the corners. Cup the mitered guard petals only enough for a round, smooth look. Wrap the edges of the guard petals with an awl to curl them toward you.

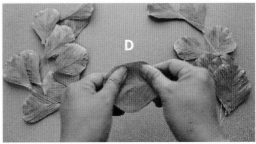

12

Note: *Because each petal is wired, you can bend them to adjust the placement. This gives you more control.*

14. **To place the petals and guard petals,** start by placing two petals like bunny ears next to the stamen and go clockwise as you place your petals. Make sure to cover your gaps as you glue your petals around the center. If you cannot see the gaps easily, turn the flower over and the gaps between the petals will be more obvious. Once you have placed all the petals, place the guard petals. Dot glue the last five guard petals evenly around the flower head base.

15. **For the leaves,** cut the two remaining 26-gauge wires in half for four 9" pieces. Seam miter the Mod Podge-painted leaf/moss crepe strip to make four leaves (as on page 22), folding with the grain every 1½", to make three leaves from Template: Peony Leaf A and one leaf from Template: Peony Leaf B.

16. **To assemble a leaf set,** arrange the four wired leaves with Leaf B in the middle, Leaf A to the right, and another Leaf A slightly below that. Wrap with floral tape to secure. Wrap down about 2" and wrap Leaf A in place. Continue taping until no wires are exposed to finish the stem.

15.

16.

139

Semi-Double Peony: Coral Charm

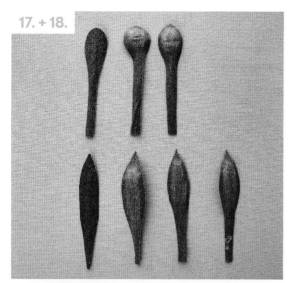

17. + 18.

19.

17. **For the sepals and bracts,** with the rest of the Mod Podge-painted leaf/moss doublette crepe, make three of Template: Peony Bracts A, three of Template: Peony Bracts B, and one of Template: Peony Bracts C, for a total of seven bracts.

18. **To shape,** cup the top third of the bracts so they are slightly concave with the Mod Podge-painted side facing out.

19. **To attach sepals to the base of the flower head,** dot the inside base of the sepals with tacky glue and attach them as follows.

> **Row 1:** two of Template: C and one of Template: B in a triangle pattern.
>
> **Row 2:** one of Template: B and two of Template: A in between the gaps of row 1.

20. **For the stem,** wrap with floral tape from the bottom of the bracts and down about 2½". Wrap to securely attach the leaf set. View from the top to make sure it can be seen from that angle. Once you are happy with the arrangement, wrap and tape to cover the remaining exposed wire and finish the stem.

Note: *A freshly bloomed peony has more petal coverage toward the center. With age, a peony's petals open more, and the carpel center is shown.*

Variation: For an Old Peony, use a scrap of German doublette crepe paper in peach/petal to make petal dye in step 1. Opt for a scrap of German doublette white/light peach or white/white to make the petals in step 11.

Double Cherry Blossom Branch

LEVEL: 7

Cherry blossoms have a special place in my heart—I even created a citywide cherry blossom event in Seattle that included six store displays in six locations. The more of these blossoms you make, the fuller and more breathtaking the branch. This tutorial will show you how to make twelve blooming blossoms on a branch, which consist of red stigma, yellow-green stamens, tiny sepals, and 144 fluffy strips of petals. Scale up for bigger arrangements or installations, or create small clusters for boutonnieres. In this tutorial, I will show you how dip-dyeing can be so versatile and easy to use to add a lovely depth to your crepe paper petals. You won't regret making this delicate blossom!

Double Cherry Blossom Branch

German extra fine crepe paper in honeysuckle

Italian crepe paper in 90 gsm 365 serpentine

German doublette crepe paper in goldenrod/buttercup

nine 22-gauge wires, cut into twelve 8" pieces, set aside the rest uncut

one 16-gauge wire, for main stem

tacky glue

floral tape or Crepe Tape (page 24) in brown

watercolor paint in medium pink (or red and white) and brush

alcohol- or water-based marker in coral

Tools: ruler, scissors, wire cutter, paintbrushes

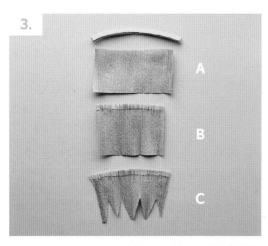

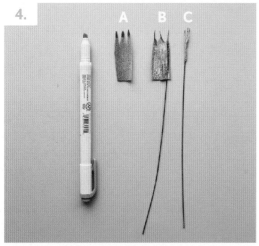

1. **To prepare the dip-dyed petal paper:** We need 144" of crepe to make twelve blossoms. So, cut against the grain to make one 144" x 3" strip of extra fine crepe in honeysuckle; accordion fold it every 12" (twelve times). Cut the folds to make twelve 12" x 3" strips. Loosely roll each of the twelve strips lengthwise.

2. **To dip-dye:** Have a cup of water handy to wet your brush and wake up the watercolor paints. To make pink, put a dab medium pink watercolor paint into a cup of water (alternatively, mix red to white in a 1:3 ratio to create pink). Dip one end of each honeysuckle crepe tube into the watercolor-dyed water for about 10 to 20 seconds. Let dry.

Note: Extra fine crepe paper is delicate when saturated with water, so move it gently and do not try to unroll until it's at least 80% dry. (See Drying, page 25, for several methods.)

5.

7. + 8.

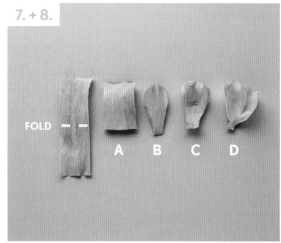

FOLD

A   B   C   D

3. **For the stamens:** To start with the filament, cut twelve 2½" x 1¾" strips of serpentine crepe. For the pollen, make twelve 2½" x ½" strips of goldenrod/buttercup doublette. Fold in half (a). Brush half the inner fold with a thin layer of tacky glue, place one strip of serpentine crepe in the middle, and glue shut to laminate (b). Let dry for a few minutes. Fringe the stamens ½" deep x ⅛" apart and then cut darts at the bottom that are ½" deep x ½" apart (as on page 18) to make twelve fringed stamen strips (c).

4. **For the pistils,** cut twelve 1" x 1¼" strips of serpentine. Cut three ¼" darts along the top edge of each. Color the tips of the darts with the coral marker (a). Twist the colored darts tightly to create the stigma. Spread glue over each darted strip (below the colored darts) (b). Place one end of an 8" wire slightly below a twisted dart and wrap the pistil strip around the wire (c). Repeat to make twelve pistils.

5. **For the centers,** dot tacky glue to attach one fringed strip of stamens slightly underneath the twisted darts around the pistil stem. Repeat to create twelve centers.

6. **For the sepals,** cut against the grain to make one 12" x 2" strip of serpentine. Accordion fold with the grain every 1" (twelve times). Cut the folds to make twelve pieces. Use Template: Cherry Sepal 1 to cut those pieces into twelve sepals.

7. **For the blossoms,** cut against the grain of the honeysuckle crepe paper to make 144 1" x 2" rectangles, twelve for each of the twelve blossoms on this branch. To make 144 petal sets, fold one strip in half against the grain (a), and place Template: Cherry Blossom 1 over it, with the folded half at the base (b). Cut to create two petals attached to each other. Fold petal set in half, and give it a ruffle (see Ruffling, page 24).

8. **To shape,** deeply cup each blossom (c). Slightly move the bottom petal to the right and twist the petal base to hold the petal set in a more opened layered position (d). Repeat to make 144 petal sets.

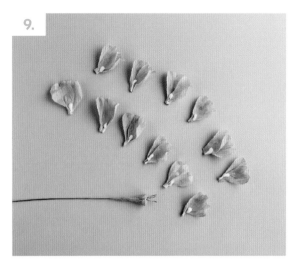

THE NEW ART OF PAPER FLOWERS

SEPAL

9. **For the blossom stems,** dot tacky glue onto the base of twelve petal sets. Layer them around a center wire in batches as follows, keeping the tops of the petals slightly higher than the stigma of the pistil stem.

> **Row 1:** Attach three petal sets around the center.
>
> **Row 2:** Attach three petal sets in the gaps created by the first layer.
>
> **Row 3:** Attach three petal sets in the gaps created by the second layer.
>
> **Row 4:** Attach three petal sets in the gaps created by the third layer.

10. Dot tacky glue on a sepal and apply it at the base of the blossom head. Repeat to put sepals on all twelve cherry blossom stems.

> *Note:* If you do not have brown floral tape, prepare brown crepe paper strips for taping. (See Crepe Tape, page 24).

11.

12.

13.

11. **To make clusters of blossoms,** start wrapping tape slightly over the green sepal and work down about 1" to create a twig. Leave a good chunk of the wires exposed so they can wrap around the main branch. Group the blossoms as you like; I created these clusters: two four-blossom clusters, one three-blossom cluster, and one loose blossom.

12. **To attach blossom clusters,** tape one four-blossom cluster to the end of the 16-gauge wire. Work the tape down the main branch about 1". Wrap the exposed blossom wire ends around the branch to create interesting knobs. Crisscross the tape to cover all exposed blossom wires. Wrap an uncut 22-gauge wire around the branch, toward the end of where you finished taping. Wrap and crisscross this wire randomly to create interesting texture along the branch, wherever you feel it needs more bulk. Add the other 22-gauge wires as needed as you work. The branch should gradually grow in diameter.

13. **To finish the branch,** cover one end of the 22-gauge wire with brown floral tape. Continue wrapping and taping down about 3" or 4" from the first blossom cluster. Attach another four-blossom cluster, tape down the main branch about 1", wrap exposed blossom wires around the branch, and tape over exposed wires. Remember to wrap and cover the 22-gauge wire along the main branch as you work down. About 2" from the last blossom cluster, attach the three-blossom cluster. Follow the same pattern, wrapping the blossom wires and covering with tape. Add brown tape to the single blossom, taping down from the green sepal about 1". About 2" from the last blossom cluster, attach the single blossom. Wrap the exposed wire and tape. Finish wrapping any exposed wires and tape up the rest of the branch. Gently bend and curve the branch to emphasize cherry blossoms.

Clematis: Florida Sieboldii

I am captivated by the center of this clematis, with its transition from creamy white to striking purple stamens, modeled after Clematis Florida Sieboldii. These flowers are notably larger than typical vine blooms, with diameters ranging from four to six inches. Note that the clematis does not have true petals; instead, it boasts vibrant sepals that mimic the appearance of petals. In most flowering plants, the petals are the colorful parts of the flower that attract pollinators like bees and butterflies. These are usually distinct from the sepals, which are typically green and serve to protect the developing bud. But the clematis's sepals have evolved to take on the appearance and function of petals. They become colorful and petal-like, while the actual petals are either reduced or absent. Their sepals are often large and vivid, and they surround the flower's reproductive parts, just as petals do in other flowers. This unique adaptation presents a thrilling artistic opportunity, allowing you to explore and recreate the clematis's beauty in your art.

Clematis: Florida Sieboldii

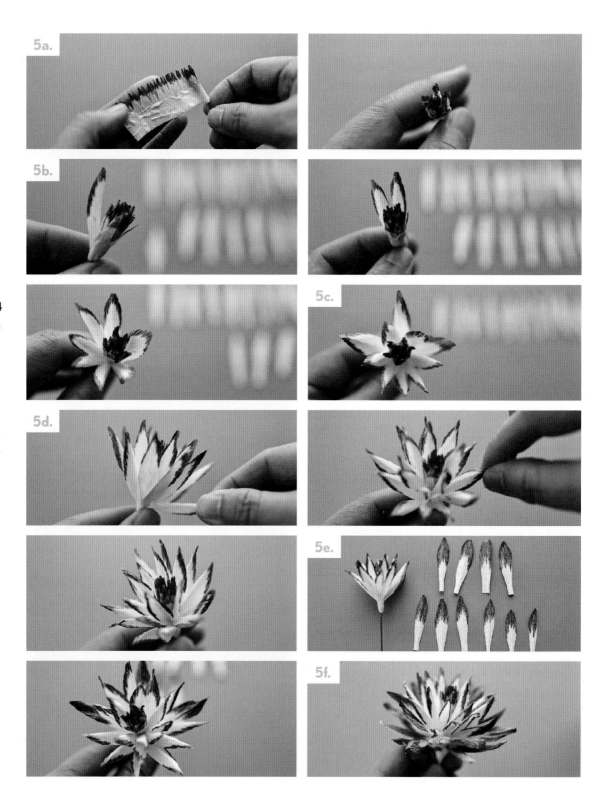

5a.

5b.

5c.

5d.

5e.

5f.

5. **To assemble the clematis,** glue and wrap the inner stamens around one end of the 20-gauge wire (a). Glue the outer stamens in rows.

> **Row 1:** Evenly glue ten of the outer stamen 1 (b).
>
> **Row 2:** In between the gaps, glue the rest of the ten outer stamen 1. When gluing these, place a tiny dot of glue and pinch the base as you place (c). This will narrow the stamen and make it look like the stamen is blooming from the center. After you finish placing the outer stamen 1, slightly twist the tip of each stamen so it is pointy and curves down (d).
>
> **Row 3:** Glue the ten outer stamen 2 in between the gaps. Slightly pinch the first few stamens and gradually lessen the pinch to make it look as if it is unfurling (e).
>
> **Rows 4 and 5:** Glue the rest of the stamens to complete the center of the clematis. Fill in gaps first and make sure the stamens are evenly distributed (f).

6. **For the sepals,** gently cup the white sepals. (See Cupping, page 17) (a). Place three of the sepals around the center at equal distance from each other (b). Place the final three sepals in between the gaps as your last row (c). Floral tape the stem. With makeup wedge sponge, apply soft pastel to the base of the sepals to blend with the tape, blending until you no longer see any loose powder (d).

6a.

6b.

6c.

6d.

English Garden Rose: Leonora

Create the elegance of an unfurling garden rose, inspired by the stunning cream-colored Leonora (Auswagsy) from David Austin Wedding Roses. If you have not experienced a garden rose in person, I highly recommend seeking them out. A garden rose can look completely different from one day to the next. Sometimes they will spiral or not. It all depends on how much sun or how warm it gets for the garden rose to do its magic. Watching them open over several days and experiencing the incredible scent will fuel your creativity. For more inspiration and to explore their entire garden rose collection, visit davidaustin.com and connect with them on social media @davidaustinweddingroses.

When crafting garden roses, embrace their imperfectly perfect nature. Focus on the graceful cup form rather than obsessing over uniform petal placement or identical cuts. Each petal can be unique in size and shape; it adds character to your creation. Feel free to hand-cut the petals for a personal touch.

This tutorial creates a cupped rosette, but you can adapt it to create a fully bloomed rose using the Miyabi tutorial in this book (page 200). Another modification is to use 90 gsm crepe stretched 60% before cutting instead of the 60 gsm paper. Usually, a garden rose has one hundred or more petals. I wanted to add the volume but not the weight, thus the lighter weight paper, but I know this is a less common weight to have on hand.

English Garden Rose: Leonora

German doublette crepe paper in leaf/moss

German doublette crepe paper in yellow/ goldenrod

German doublette crepe paper in white/white

Italian crepe paper in 60 gsm 330 white

three 6" 26-gauge wires

one 18-gauge wire

tacky glue

Mod Podge in matte

floral tape or Crepe Tape (page 24) in dark green

soft pastel in yellow, such as PanPastel in yellow ocher tint 270.8

Tools: ruler, scissors, wire cutter, paintbrush, makeup brush

Note: Finding real garden rose specimens to study can be challenging, due to the prevalence of hybrid roses at florists and grocery stores; most of the time, you must search online for detailed images. Websites like davidaustin.com are invaluable for exploring the intricate details of garden roses. Their site offers high-quality close-ups, essential for artists and gardeners who need to study petal arrangements and color gradations for projects or garden planning. David Austin is renowned for breeding some of the most beautiful garden roses in the world. Their website provides high-quality, close-up photographs of their rose varieties, which can be incredibly helpful. These images allow for a detailed examination of the characteristics that make each garden rose variety unique—from the depth and richness of colors to the complexity of petal shapes. By studying these close-ups, you can appreciate the nuances of each variety and better understand how to replicate their beauty in your work.

1. **To prepare the matte-painted paper,** cut against the grain to make one 6½" x 3" strip and one 3¾" x 4" strip of leaf/moss doublette crepe. Brush to coat one side of all three strips with matte Mod Podge (page 23). Let dry, 1 to 3 hours.

2. **For the stamens,** use one 1½" x 2½" strip of white/white doublette crepe and one 1½" x 1" strip of goldenrod/buttercup doublette crepe, laminating and fringing (as on page 19) only slightly past the yellow edge, about ¼".

3. **For the inner petals,** cut against the grain to make eight 10" x 2" strips of white/white doublette crepe.

4. **To color,** on one side of each strip firmly but lightly brush to apply soft pastel in yellow. Do not color the entire strip; just give a hint of yellow. Rub with the grain. The color is set when you do not see any more loose powder. Accordion fold each strip with the grain every 1¼" (eighty times). Cut the folds to make eighty pieces.

5. **To shape,** use Template: Leonora 1 to cut those eighty pieces into petals. Stretch the top fourth of each petal. Set aside thirty of these to attach to the flower head as loose inner petals (step 14).

Tip: When stretching petals, you can go faster by stretching three or more at a time. See Stretching (page 24) for more.

6. **For the layered inner petals,** group the remaining fifty inner petals into ten five-petal sets. To layer each five-petal set, place a dot of glue at the base of four petals, and layer these four behind an unglued petal, but as you place each petal, fold it in half and make sure each one sits differently, peeking out about ⅛" at the top, left, or right. (This creates small air pockets so individual petals can be seen as the viewer looks at the rose's center.)

7. Cup the bottom third of the set to separate the petals a bit. Repeat to create ten five-petal sets.

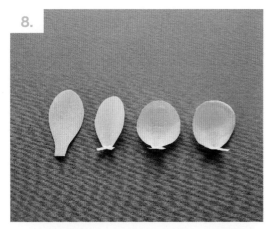

8.

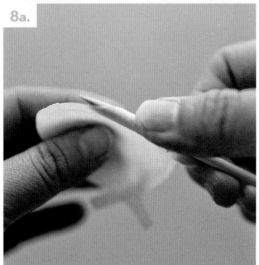

8a.

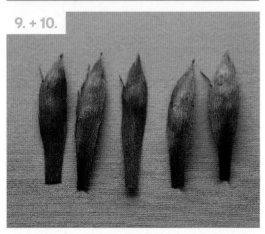

9. + 10.

8. **For the outer petals,** cut against the grain to make one 36" x 3" strip of white/white doublette crepe. Accordion fold with the grain every 1½" (twenty-four times). Cut along the folds to make twenty-four pieces. Use Template: Leonora 2 to cut them into twenty-four petals. Cut a 1" slit in the center of the base of each petal.

Place a dot of glue to the right of the slit. Cross the base to the left of the slit, forming an X. This will help create that deep cup. Repeat with all the petals. Cup the base of each petal right above the slit, and slowly move upward to form a more rounded and upright look. With an awl, curl out the tips of the petals (a).

9. **For the calyxes,** grab the Mod Podge-painted 3¾" x 4" strip of leaf/moss doublette crepe. Accordion fold with the grain every ¾" (five times). Cut the folds to make five pieces. With Template: Leonora Calyx, cut those into five calyxes. Along both sides of each calyx, cut two or three ¼" to ½" darts. Choose which green (leaf or moss) you want facing the viewer. I like the brighter green (leaf) showing as it is a freshly bloomed rose; choose the darker green (moss) for an older bloom.

10. **To shape,** slightly cup the center of each calyx starting from the top middle and then down, cupping inward on the darker green side if you want to make the lighter green pop more. Twist the top of each cupped calyx to make the tip more pointed, and twist each of the darts on the edges.

Tip: If you find the tip hard to twist, trim the point so it is slimmer and easier to twist.

11. **To finish the leaves and stem:** Use the 6½" x 3" strip of Mod Podge-painted leaf/moss doublette crepe and Template: Rose Leaf 1 to miter three leaves (as on page 22). Cut in a bit of sawtooth edging, although this variety has fewer ridges than many other roses. Wire with the 26-gauge pieces and leave the wire tails long.

Tip: For a longer stem, consider adding a five-leaflet set to the rose stem. Alternatively, omit the leaves or put them on their own stem for floral arrangements.

12. Floral tape down a leaf stem about 1¾". Tape two more leaves onto the first stem. The leaves should sit opposite one another.

Note: When placing your petals, keep in mind that the rose is blooming and that you want to echo petals as they bloom (see page 61). So, each petal should be placed sequentially in the petal line. You can also interlace petals in between the earlier petal sets so the petals will bloom more seamlessly. The more tightly the petals are placed, the more budlike you will make the rose. The more loosely you glue the petal set, the more bloomed your garden rose will be.

13. **To assemble the center,** evenly add tacky glue to the lower half of the stamen strip. Wrap the stamen around the 18-gauge wire (a). Glue the ten inner petal sets around the stamen, with

13a.

13b.

13c.

13d.

14.

the tips of the petals sitting about 1" above the pollen (b). Press the sets in half as you glue (c). A good starting place is adding two sets side by side, like bunny ears, then continuing around. Do not worry about precision. Keep the center loose and open, but let it be unique (d).

14. **To attach petals to the flower head,** add the thirty loose inner petals, gluing them around the blooming center in approximately three rows. That means you should go around the bloom once for every ten petals you add. Place these at the same height as the inner petal sets. Add glue to the lower third of each outer petal, on both sides. This will help the petal stand upright. Place nineteen of the outer petals around the center in at least three rows, as you did with the inner petals. With the last five petals, spread them out equally for the last layer.

15. **To finish the stem:** Tacky glue the five calyxes around the base of the rose head. Floral tape around the base of the rose and down the stem about 3½". Tape on the leaflet set and wrap to the end of the stem.

For a **Fully Bloomed English Garden Rose,** follow this tutorial through step 4 and use steps 4–7 from the Miyabi tutorial (page 200), and use 90 gsm crepe stretched 60% before cutting instead of the 60 gsm paper.

Tulip

In the past I have always made my tulips with German doublette crepe paper, but I want to show you how versatile the 90 gsm Italian crepe paper can be. Because it is made with high-quality, nontoxic dye, you can soak it in water to create your own custom dye that can be used or bottled and saved for later. Known for their wide variety of stunning color combinations and multicolor petals, tulips are ideal for experimenting with color. I make an orange-tipped yellow tulip in this tutorial. A tulip's petals and sepals look the same, and so they are known as tepals. Refer to the chart on page 171 to make tulips in a variety of striking color variations.

In addition to explaining how to turn scraps of crepe paper into dye, this tutorial shows how to build up the structure of a flower head that consists of the pistil (stigma, style, and ovary) and the stamen (anther and filament) and how they connect. You will find that 75% of the time you will be focused on making these dainty centers of the tulip, and it does not take long to make the big, brightly colored tepals. The Parrot Tulip and Peony Tulip (pages 172 and 176) follow this basic method as well. Master this tulip, and you can create a wide variety of stunning blooms.

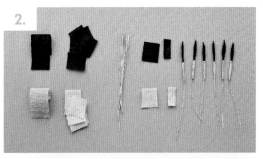

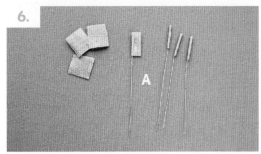

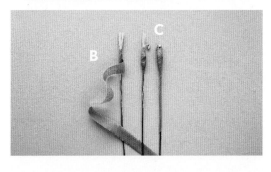

1. **To prepare the paper,** cut against the grain to make one 21" x 3½" strip of Tuscany yellow crepe. Roll the strip loosely like a cannoli. Add a scrap of orange crepe to ½ cup water; let it soak until all the orange has leached out of the paper. Remove and discard the scrap. Dip the rolled yellow crepe into the orange water. Let the orange absorb up the sides about 1". (See page 118 for a photo of this technique used for a poppy.) Flip the roll to dip the other end in the orange water, letting it soak up about 1" again. Take it out of the water and flip. Let it dry upside-down so the last color will run down. Optional: Add white details while the crepe is still wet. This white is subtle, so the orange paint can be prominent. Add about ½ cup water to a tablespoon of white paint and mix well. With a brush, dab some of the white paint on the edge of the crepe paper and let it slightly run down the sides. Repeat dabbing on the other end. Let dry.

2. **For the pollen,** cut against the grain to make one 2" x ¾" strip blackberry crepe. Stretch it 100%. Cut the stretched strip into six ¾" squares (depending on how much you stretched, you may have some remaining).

3. To create the effect of pollen-tipped wires, work one at a time. Put a line of glue on a square and brush to spread it into a thin layer. Fold the square in half with the grain. Put another line of glue across the folded square and brush to spread it into a thin layer.

4. Add a 26-gauge wire to one side and trifold it closed (meaning, place the wire in the middle third of the strip and fold the two sides over it). Pinch the top and bottom to shape the pollen into an oval shape. With an awl, imprint a line in the middle on one side of the oval. Cut with the grain to make one 2½" x ¾" strip of yellow mustard. Stretch it 100%. Cut the stretched strip into nine ¾" squares.

5. Attach one square of stretched mustard crepe to each pollen-tipped wire. Put a line of glue on one square and brush to spread it into a thin layer. Fold the square in half with the grain. Put another line of glue on the folded square and spread into a thin layer. Place one square of stretched mustard crepe below the pollen part of wire, with the wire to one side, and the trifold closed. Pinch the top and bottom. Flatten the middle. Repeat to make six pollen-tipped wires.

6d.

6e.

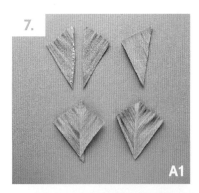

7.

A1

7. + 8.

A2

B

C1

C2

Note: *For a cleaner looking stamen, you can trim any extra bits away with scissors and reshape the pollen and filament, so it is smoother looking.*

6. **For the stigma,** place a thin layer of glue on the last three mustard squares. Wrap each strip around a 26-gauge wire. Place the 20-gauge wire in the middle of these three wires (a). The top of the 20-gauge should sit near the bottom of the yellow paper. Starting at the bottom of the yellow, tape the four wires together (b). Build up bulk by crisscrossing the tape in an X motion. Taper the top and bottom to make it bulbous shaped. Once you are satisfied with the style, finish floral taping down to where the shorter wires end. Roll the exposed yellow tips twice each with your fingers, bending outward from the center (c). This will help taper the tips more easily. Take your six pollen-tipped wires and place them evenly around the stigma wire. Floral tape them together and make sure the pollen tips are about ¼" higher than the stigma (d). Then with your index and thumb, slightly bend the base of the pollen tip wires so that they gently curve up and outward (e).

7. **For the tepals,** unroll the dry strip of dip-dyed crepe. Cut six 2½" pieces; set aside the remaining 6" piece. Overlap miter the six 2½" pieces with wire (page 23) to make six tepals using Template: Tulip 1 and six 7" wires (a1). Out of the remaining 6" strip, cut twelve ½" strips. Cut to taper and round one end of each strip; this end will be glued to the top of the tepal.

8. **To shape the tepals,** put two lines of glue down the sides of each strip. Glue two strips on each tepal, covering the middle wire bump, front and back (a2). Cut two parallel vertical slits about 1" into the base of each tepal, dividing the base into thirds; this will allow you to form a deep cup (b). Turn one so the grain is vertical and slowly stretch and deeply cup the tepal (c1). See Cupping (page 17) for more info. With an awl, curl in the tepals' tips (c2).

9. **To attach petals to the flower head,** glue three tepals (equally spaced) around the center, with the stamen tops slightly above the midpoint of each tepal. Use the outer tabs from the slits on each tepal to hug around the wire, with the middle tab glued straight down the stem. Take the final three tepals and glue them in between the gaps created by the first row. If needed, re-curl the tepals and adjust as needed.

10. **For the stem,** measure the wire against the clear plastic tubing. Cut the tubing to the size of your wire. Insert the stem into the plastic tube. To make a clean edge from the base of the tulip head to the plastic tube, wrap with floral tape; to make this easier, start the tape on the plastic tube and floral tape around the top of it. Build up tape in the gap between the tube and the base of the tulip head. When you reach the base, wrap evenly around it once or twice to secure; check that it is tight before taping back down the plastic tube stem for a seamless transition. Wrap to the bottom of the stem with floral tape. Reshape the stem so it curves the way you like, and you are done!

German Doublette Tulip: German doublette crepe paper is a fantastic material for creating tulips; however, it is important to note that the dyeing process reacts differently with this type of paper compared to 90 gsm Italian crepe. When using German doublette crepe, the absorption of colors results in softer, more blended lines than the distinctive lines you see with 90 gsm Italian crepe. This difference can create a more subtle but equally beautiful effect. I encourage you to experiment with both crepe paper types and see these variations in color dynamics. Try using each method and let me know which one you prefer! Keep exploring and trying new techniques, allowing yourself to personalize each flower according to your creative vision. As we dive into the nuances of crafting tulips from different types of crepe paper, remember the endless possibilities these techniques can bring to your floral projects.

Tulips in a World of Color

Tulip tepal (petal) and stamen colors come in exquisite pairings, whether they complement or contrast each other. Refer to the following chart to make tulips in a variety of striking color variations.

TEPALS (PETALS)	STAMENS
red	black or almost dark purple
yellow	bright yellow to light orange
white	bright yellow to lime green
purple	dark purple to black
pink	bright yellow to light orange
orange	bright yellow to bright orange

Parrot Tulip

The beautiful thing about parrot tulips is the amount and variety of colors in one tepal, or petal. To achieve this effect, I dip-dye crepe paper. The longer you leave crepe paper in water, the more color will leach out. In this project, I use the white paint and water method. I let the crepe paper sit in the white water, and two things happen: the orange in the crepe leaches out, and the white paint is absorbed in, giving you a nice yellow-to-orange ombre effect. You can do this with an assortment of crepe paper colors. Mix it up and play around to get the fun parrot tulips!

This Parrot Tulip tutorial uses the same basic method as the Tulip, page 164, with the addition of fringing and a new coloring method.

Parrot Tulip

Italian crepe paper in 90 gsm 389 blackberry

Italian crepe paper in 90 gsm 376 yellow mustard

Italian crepe paper in 90 gsm 374 orange

one 20-gauge wire

six 7" 26-gauge petal wires

nine 3 ½" 26-gauge center wires

clear plastic tubing (³⁄₁₆")

tacky glue

floral tape or Crepe Tape (page 24) in medium green

watercolor or gouache paint in white

acrylic paint or paper scraps

Tools: ruler, scissors, wire cutter, awl, brush

174

1. **For the tepals,** follow Tepals section of the Tulip tutorial (page 164) to make six tepals, with these changes:

   In step 1, cut a 21" x 3½" strip of orange Italian crepe (not yellow). Color the ½ cup of dip water with 1 tablespoon white paint (instead of a scrap of crepe).

   In step 7, use Template: Parrot Tulip 1 for the overlap mitered tepals.

   In step 8, before cupping, randomly add two to four 1" to 1½" deep diagonal cuts to both sides of each tepal. Fringe ¼" to ½" deep along the edges. Turn tepal tops toward you, and with your scissors at a 45-degree angle, make random ⅛" cuts against the fringe for a more feather-like texture.

2. **To assemble and finish stem,** follow the instructions for that of the Tulip (page 169).

Peony Tulip

Like the exotic parrot tulip, this peony tulip features striking variegated lines on its tepals, a characteristic that contributes significantly to its visual appeal. The tutorial begins with dip-dyeing the crepe paper to replicate this beautiful effect. This foundational layer of color creates a vibrant base, to which you can add layers of color. To introduce distinctive variegated lines that mimic the peony tulip's natural gradients, you will carefully drip paint onto the already-dyed paper. This technique allows for precision in adding unique streaks and enhances the depth and texture of each tepal. Moreover, adding a slight ombre effect toward the edges of the tepals deepens the realism and turns this bloom into a truly show-stopping piece. This method of layering color and texture invites drama and delicacy into your floral arrangement, giving each peony tulip a unique bloom.

Peony Tulip

Italian crepe paper in 90 gsm 385 rose quartz

Italian crepe paper in 90 gsm 389 blackberry

Italian crepe paper in 90 gsm 376 yellow mustard

nine 3 ½" 26-gauge wires for center wires

fifteen 7" 30-gauge wires for petal wires

one 20-gauge wire

clear plastic tubing (³⁄₁₆")

tacky glue

floral tape or Crepe Tape (page 24) in medium green

watercolor or gouache paint in white and dark pink (or red and white)

Tools: ruler, scissors, gloves, paintbrush, wire cutter, awl

8a.

8b.

1. **To prepare the dip-dyed paper,** cut against the grain to make one 45" x 3½" strip of rose quartz crepe. Roll the strip loosely like a cannoli.

2. **To dip-dye,** mix to combine about ½ cup water with 1 tablespoon white paint. (I put on gloves at this point to avoid staining my fingers.) Dip one end of the rolled rose quartz crepe into the white water. (See page 118 for a photo of this dip-dying process.) Let some of the pink color seep out and the white soak in to create an ombre effect. Leave it in until you're happy with the color transformation.

3. Flip the roll to dip the other end, letting it soak until you are happy with the color. Take it out of the water and flip to dry upside-down so the color runs down.

4. **To add another color layer,** optional: While the rolled crepe is still wet, add subtle details

in white; mix to combine ½ cup water with 1 tablespoon white paint. With a brush, dab some of the white paint on the edge of the crepe paper and let it run down. Repeat, dabbing on the other end.

5. For the second layer of color, add a small, dime-size amount of dark pink paint to ¼ cup water. (Alternatively, mix white and red paint to create pink.) While the rolled crepe is still wet, brush pink water onto both ends. Let it drip varying lengths. Let dry (see Drying, page 25).

6. **For the core,** follow the core section of the Tulip tutorial (page 164) to create the foundation of this tulip.

7. **For the tepals,** unroll the dry dip-dye-painted strip of crepe. Cut fifteen 2" pieces; set aside the remaining 15". Overlap miter (as described on page 23) to make fifteen tepals, using Template: Peony Tulip 1 to cut six tepals and using Template: Peony Tulip 2 to cut nine tepals. Tacky glue one 7" wire in each flap. With the remaining 15" strip, cut thirty narrow strips each ½" wide. With scissors, taper and round one end of each strip. Add two lines of glue down the sides of each strip. Glue two strips on each tepal, covering the middle wire bump, front and back. Cut two parallel slits about 1" long at the base of each tepal. This will allow you to form a deep cup.

8. **To shape the tepals,** turn the tepal so the grain is vertical and slowly stretch and deeply cup the tepal (a). With an awl, curl in the tepals' tips (b). For added strength, put thin lines of tacky

glue inside of the tepals. Without stretching the crepe, rub the glue into the crepe line with your thumb (c). Let dry. Cup the dry tepals one more time and slightly bend the wire to curve naturally (d).

9. **To assemble,** attach tepals in rows, and as you glue each one, use its two outer tabs to hug the stem; glue the middle tab straight down the stem.

> **Row 1:** Glue three of the Template: Peony Tulip 1 tepals equally around the center.
>
> **Row 2:** Glue three more Template: Peony Tulip 1 tepals in the gaps of the first row.
>
> **Row 3:** Glue three of the Template: Peony Tulip 2 tepals in the gaps of the second row.
>
> **Row 4:** Glue three more Template: Peony Tulip 2 tepals in the gaps of the third row.
>
> **Row 5:** Glue three more Peony Tulip 2 tepals in the gaps of the fourth row.
>
> *Note:* With your index finger and thumb, reach in and readjust the tepals so they curve up naturally. If needed, re-curl and adjust your tepals.

9.

ROW 1

10. **To finish the stem,** measure the wire against the plastic tube and cut the plastic to size. Insert the stem into the plastic tube. Floral tape a clean edge from the base of the tulip head to the plastic tube. To make it easier, start right on the plastic tube and floral tape around that area. Build up the gap. When you get to the base of the tulip head, go around once or twice in an even, straight line and make sure it is tight around the base before going back down again. It is a seamless transition from tulip head to plastic tube. Finish floral taping down the tube. Reshape the stem so it curves the way you like, and you are done!

SIDE VIEW
ROW 2

ROW 2

ROW 3

ROW 4

SIDE VIEW
ROW 4

ROW 5

10.

Zinnia: Zinderella Peach

LEVEL: 8

The ruffly petals of the Zinderella Peach variety of zinnia are evocative of a ballerina's delicate, flowing tutu. This resemblance stems from the zinnia's long outer petals and fluffy shorter petals that encircle the central disc. To create the soft color of these tutu-like petals, I use a color washing technique.

This zinnia's center disc is densely packed with smaller disc florets, some of which are open and others that stay tightly closed. Small bracts that gracefully uphold the flower head add structural support to this captivating floral display. The entire bloom is perched atop a robust stem, flanked by pairs of vibrant green leaves, enhancing its visual appeal and mimicking the zinnia's natural growth.

As you assemble everything from the intricately layered petals to the lush, green foliage, you will capture the physical beauty of the flower and embody the graceful poise of a ballet dancer in bloom.

Zinnia: Zinderella Peach

Italian crepe paper in 90 gsm 356 peach, or any peach or apricot color

Italian crepe paper in 90 gsm 366 olive

German doublette crepe paper in yellow/goldenrod

German doublette crepe paper in white/peach

German doublette crepe paper in leaf/moss

thirty-six 3" 26-gauge wires for the floret stems

four 6" 26-gauge wires for the leaf stems

one 18-gauge paper-covered wire

tacky glue

floral tape or Crepe Tape (page 24) in medium green

watercolor paint in yellow and red

purple alcohol marker, such as Copic

one spun cotton ball (6 mm)

Tools: awl, ruler, scissors, wire cutter, paintbrushes, scalloped pinking shears (3 mm)

2.

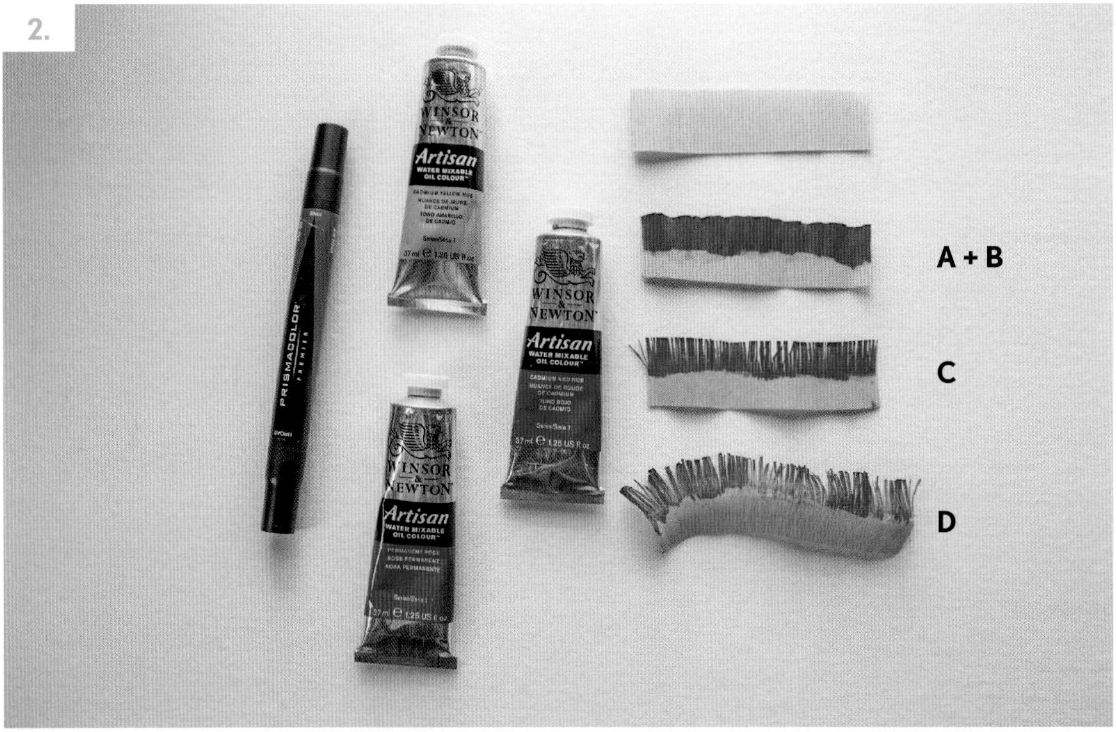

A + B

C

D

1. **To prepare the washed crepe,** wash yellow doublette crepe to create varying shades of yellows. Let dry (see washing methods on page 25).

2. **For the unopened disc florets,** cut against the grain to make four 4" x 1" strips of yellow/goldenrod doublette crepe. Wet a paintbrush and mix yellow and red in a 1:3 ratio to create a dark orangey-red. Paint the bottom half of one strip with orange-red watercolor (a). Let dry. Deepen the color of your painted strip by applying thin lines (about ⅛") of purple alcohol marker along the top edge (b). Fringe all four strips about halfway down (c). With the back of your scissors, bend the middle of each strip at a 45-degree angle (d).

3. **For the opened disc florets,** cut against the grain to make one 12" x ½" strip of yellow/goldenrod doublette crepe. Stretch 100% to make the strip 36". Accordion fold with the grain every 1" (thirty-six times). Cut the folds to make thirty-six 1" x ½" strips. Dot each of the strips with tacky glue and wrap around one end of a 3" wire to form a slim oval top.

4. **For the (unopened and opened) petal strips,** cut against the grain to make one 22" x 1¼" strip of washed crepe. With scalloped pinking shears, cut along the top of the strip to scallop the edge. Fringe ¼" in between the scallops to create petal edges. Count out five petals and cut into individual strips. You should have thirty-six of them. Trim the sides of the petal strips at a 45-degree angle to reduce bulk.

4.

Apply glue to the bottom half of the floret and wrap around the oval top stems. Open the petals to look like little stars. Make thirty-six. Set aside.

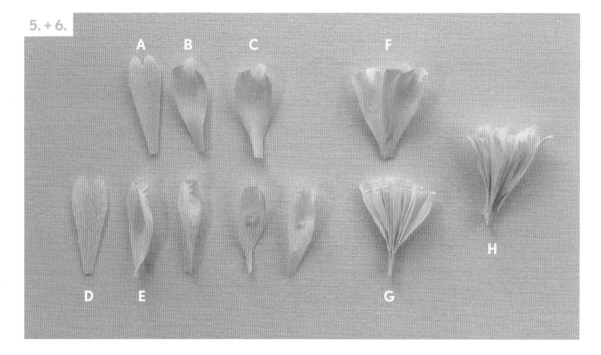

5. **For the spoon-shaped ray florets,** cut the white/peach German doublette crepe into a 49" x 2" strip (this is about the length of one roll of doublette crepe). Cut the strip with the grain into forty-eight petals with Template: Zinnia Petal 1 (a). Cup the middle of the petals, making sure the peach color is facing you (b). Slightly ruffle the top of each petal (c). Cut against the grain to make one 40" x 2" strip of 90 gsm peach crepe. Stretch until it doubles in length. Cut the strip with the grain into eighty petals with Template: Zinnia Petal 2 (d).

6. **To shape,** cup the middle of the petals (e). Add small ruffles to the tops. For Petal Set 1: take 3 petals of Petal 1, dot glue at the base of each petal, and glue overlapping each other so they look like a fan (f). Make sixteen sets. To make Petal Set 2: take 5 petals of Petal 2, dot glue at the base of the petal, fold them in half, and glue side by side so they look like a ruffle fan (g). Make sixteen sets. To combine Petal Set 1 with Petal Set 2: glue one set of Petal 2 set on top of the base of Petal 1 (h).

7. **For the petaloid ray florets,** cut with the grain to make a 2⅜" tall strip from the roll of white/peach doublette crepe. Cut twelve petals with Template: Zinnia Petal 3. From underneath, smooth the petal with your finger to iron any wrinkles. Run your thumbnail down the middle to create a raised line on the top. With an awl, carefully curl up the petal tops.

8. **For the bracts,** cut one 5" x 1½" strip of olive crepe. Use the scalloped pinking shears along the top edge, then fringe ⅛" between the scallops to create petal edges. Fold the strip into thirds with the grain, and cut to create three even pieces.

9. **For the leaves:** Using the brighter (leaf-colored) side of the leaf/moss doublette crepe, Template: Zinnia Leaf, and four 4" stem wires, seam miter to make four wired leaves as on page 22.

10. + 11.

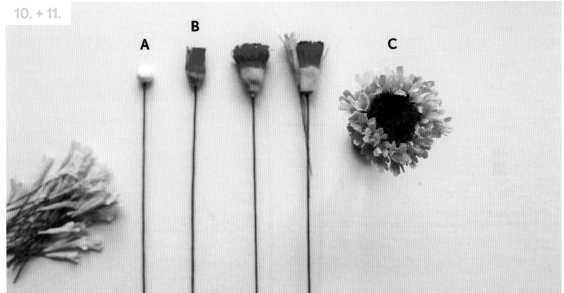

A   B   C

10. **For the core,** glue a spun cotton ball onto the main stem wire. Let it dry 100% (a).

11. **To assemble the flower head,** apply lines of tacky glue to all four strips of the unopened disc florets, and attach them around the spun cotton ball (b). Glue the thirty-six opened disc florets around the unopened disc florets (c). Glue slightly above so they are floating on top. Use as little glue as possible, otherwise it will not dry well. Alternatively, you can use floral tape. Make sure the florets are even around the center. Glue the sixteen sets of spoon-shaped

D

ray florets around the center (d). Make sure these sets are full and even all around. Take the time to fluff out the spoon-shaped ray florets, separating the individual florets so they are not mushed together. You want the florets to be full and fluffy. Glue the twelve petaloid ray florets beneath (e). Glue the bracts strips around the base of the flower head. As you go around the flower, make sure each scalloped strip is slightly lowered so you can see each row. Depending how tight you glue the strips, you should have three to four rows.

12. **To finish the foliage and stem,** floral tape to cover the bottom fourth of bracts. Slightly cup a rounded bowl shape into the leaves. About 4" down from the flower head, attach the first set of two leaves facing each other and secure with floral tape. Wrap tape about 2½" down the stem, and tape to attach the next two leaves. This leaf set should sit between the other one so that when you look down at the flower from above, the two leaf sets form a plus sign. Finish taping the stem, and you are done.

E

BRACT

12.

Dahlia: Terracotta

If you appreciate the beauty of symmetry, you will thoroughly enjoy crafting the intricate petal formations of a dahlia. Celebrated for their impressive diversity in color, shape, and size, dahlias are a fascinating subject for any paper flower artist. This tutorial is inspired by the variety Terracotta, known for its slightly unusual petal structure. Once you master it, you will have no trouble altering petal shapes to create a wide array of varieties from the vast and vibrant world of dahlias cultivated globally. As you delve into this project, you will also learn several crucial techniques in paper flower creation. These include strategies for filling in gaps to ensure lush, full blooms, effectively managing the placement and attachment of multiple petals, and the importance of using just the right amount of glue for secure yet subtle adhesion. These lessons will enhance your skills and broaden your understanding, helping you create stunningly realistic and artistically fulfilling floral arrangements.

To hold this flower's petals—all eighty of them—in place, you need a paper-craft mechanism at the core that serves as the base foundation. In comes the spun cotton ball. This hidden support structure stabilizes the petals in the precise, tessellated pattern of the natural, dense arrangement found in real dahlias. The result is a flower with a lush, full appearance but controlled complexity. This simple spun cotton technique enhances the paper dahlia's overall durability and aesthetic appeal, making it an impressive addition to any floral arrangement or display.

Dahlia: Terracotta

German doublette crepe paper in leaf/moss

German doublette crepe paper in white/white

German doublette crepe paper in honeysuckle/coral

one 26-gauge wire, cut into thirds about 6" each

one 18-gauge wire, for main stem

spun cotton ball (6 mm)

tacky glue

glue stick

floral tape or Crepe Tape (page 24) in dark green

Mod Podge in gloss

watercolor paints in red, yellow, and green

Tools: ruler, scissors, flat paintbrush, awl

192

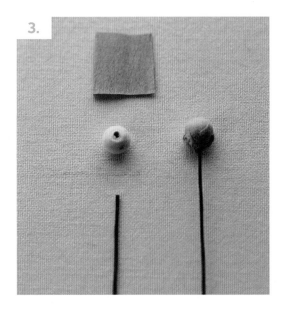

3.

1. **For the gloss Mod Podge-painted paper,** cut against the grain to make one 12" x 3" strip and one 4½" x 2½" strip of leaf/moss doublette crepe. Brush a coat of gloss Mod Podge onto whichever side you want to show. Let dry, 1 to 3 hours.

2. **For the gloss- and watercolor-painted paper,** cut with the grain to make one 2½" x 2" strip of white/white doublette crepe. Brush a coat of gloss Mod Podge on one side. Let dry, 1 to 3 hours. Wet a paintbrush and mix yellow and green watercolor to create light olive green. Brush light olive green onto the Mod Podge-painted side of the white/white strip. Let dry.

4.

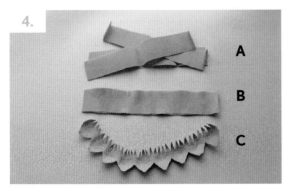

A

B

C

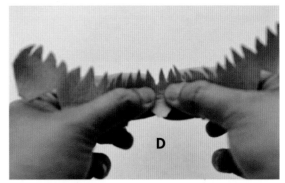

D

5.

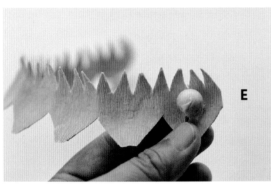

E

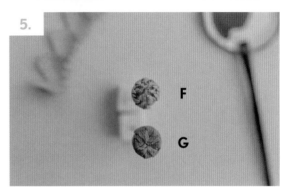

F

G

3. **For the core,** tacky glue the spun cotton ball onto one end of the 18-gauge wire. Cut one 1" square of honeysuckle/coral crepe paper. Tacky glue down over the spun cotton with the lighter (coral) side facing out.

4. Cut three 8" x 1½" strips of honeysuckle/coral crepe (a). Use a glue stick to laminate two of the strips together, lighter (honeysuckle) sides facing in. Glue the third strip on top of the laminated strip, darker (coral) side facing out (b). Cut about eight ½" x ½" darts along one edge of the laminated strips to prevent bulk when glued to the stem. On the opposite edge cut ¼" x ¼" darts to form the petal points for the center of the flower (c); before the glue

dries, carefully cup down the center of the strip and curve in, in preparation to fit around the spun cotton ball (d). Put lines of tacky glue on the lower half of the lighter (honeysuckle) side. Wrap tightly around the spun cotton ball, darker (coral) side facing out (e). Let dry.

5. **To assemble,** gently press the top petal points down into the center (f). Paint the center a darker pinkish/red with watercolor (g). You can use more than one wash of watercolor if needed to darken the color, but remember, less is more, as water dilutes the glue. Let dry.

6.

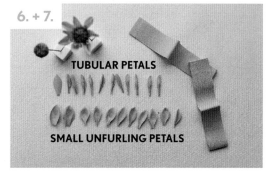

6. + 7.

TUBULAR PETALS

SMALL UNFURLING PETALS

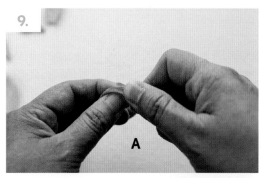

9.

A

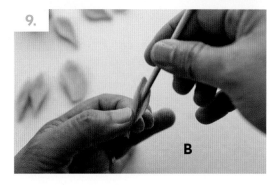

9.

B

6. **For the tubular petals,** cut against the grain to make one 6" x 1½" strip of honeysuckle/coral crepe. Accordion fold with the grain every ½" (twelve times). Cut the folds to make twelve pieces. Use Template: Dahlia 1 to cut those pieces into twelve petals. With the darker (coral) color facing you, cup the center of each petal and roll into tubes.

7. **For the small unfurling petals,** cut against the grain to make one 20" x 1½" strip of honeysuckle/coral. Accordion fold with the grain every 2" (ten times). Cut the folds to make ten pieces. Use Template: Dahlia 2 to cut those pieces into ten petals. Slightly cup and roll all ten small, unfurling petals until tubular, the lighter (honeysuckle) side facing out.

8. **For the medium unfurling petals,** cut against the grain to make one 10" x 1½" strip of honeysuckle /coral. Accordion fold with the grain every 1" (ten times). Cut the folds to make ten pieces. Use Template: Dahlia 3 to cut these into ten medium petals. Cup the centers. With the flat edge of a pair of scissors, curl out the top third and sides of each petal. To create a small, rolled opening for each petal, put the awl about 1" from the base, and use your thumb and index finger to pinch the base of the petal while twisting the awl.

9. **For the large unfurling petals,** cut with the grain to make one 12" x 2½" strip of honeysuckle/coral. Use Template: Dahlia 4 to cut twelve petals. Reverse cup them with the lighter (honeysuckle) side facing you. Run your thumb down the center to smooth any wrinkles

or lines. Curl the left edge of each petal around the pointed end of an awl (a). To create a small, rolled opening, put the awl about 1" from the base, and use your thumb and index finger to pinch the base while twisting the awl (b).

10. **For the inner petals,** cut with the grain to make one 20" x 2½" strip of honeysuckle/coral. Accordion fold with the grain every 1" (twenty times). Cut the folds. Use Template: Dahlia 5 to cut out twenty inner petals. Slightly cup the lighter (honeysuckle) side of each petal from tip to base. Fold in the sides ¼" and crease down one-third from the top of each petal. Cup the petal bases.

11. **For the outer petals,** cut with the grain to make one 20" x 3" strip of honeysuckle/coral. Accordion fold with the grain every 1¼" (sixteen times). Cut the folds. Use Template: Dahlia 6 to cut out sixteen outer petals. Slightly cup their lighter (honeysuckle) sides from tip to base (a). Fold in the sides ¼" and crease one-third down. Cup the bases, which will bend up the petals (b). Put two small tacky glue dots at the base of each petal to glue down sides.

11a.

11b.

Dahlia: Terracotta

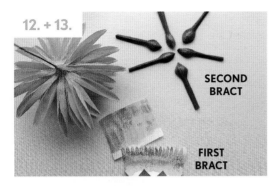

12. + 13.

SECOND BRACT

FIRST BRACT

14.

12. **For the first bract set,** cut multiple small ¼" wide by ¾" deep darts into ¼" edge of the light olive-painted strip of crepe. On the other edge, cut five bigger darts (½" x ½") to lessen the bulk when wrapped around the main stem. Stretch the strip 60%, slightly separating the darts. Run a thumbnail over the unpainted side of each dart with your index finger reinforcing underneath to lightly cup each dart in the stretched strip. Bend the bracts up 90 degrees with the painted side facing up.

13. **For the second bract set,** use Template: Dahlia 7 to cut six bracts out of the 4½" x 2 ½" strip of Mod Podge-painted leaf/moss crepe. Slightly cup all six bracts on the side not painted with Mod Podge. With the pointed end of the awl, curl the left and right sides of the bracts.

14. **For the leaflet set,** seam miter (as on page 22) using the 12" x 3" strip of Mod Podge-painted leaf/moss to make one leaf from Template: Dahlia Leaf 1 and two leaves from Template: Dahlia Leaf 2. Slightly cup the left and right side of each leaf. Floral tape about 1" down the large leaf, and then add the other two leaves. Floral tape to finish the leaflet set.

Note: I am right-handed, so I cut round corners on all the right sides, then flip over and cut all the right sides again. If you are left-handed, you may find it more comfortable to do the opposite.

SET 1

SET 2

SET 3

SIDE VIEW

SET 4

SET 4

SET 5

SET 6

16.

17.

15. **To attach petals to the flower head,** grab the main stem and make sure the point of the center is facing down. If not, press it down. Attach the petals in the order you made them:

> **Set 1:** Apply twelve petals from Template: Dahlia 1. Place lines of tacky glue on the lower half of the center. Position and glue the tubular petals around the center. Make sure they sit slightly higher than the center, ranging from ¼" to ½".

> **Set 2:** Apply ten petals from Template: Dahlia 2. Place thin lines of glue on the bottom part of the more cylindrical unfurling small petals. Place randomly around the center, pinching the base and pressing the petals to the center as you go.

> **Set 3:** Apply ten petals from Template: Dahlia 3. Add thin lines of glue to the bottom part of the rest of the unfurling small petals. Place randomly around the center, pinching the base and filling any gaps left from the petals applied earlier. Make sure these petals start extending out ¼" as you glue around the center.

> **Set 4:** Apply twelve petals from Template: Dahlia 4. With the unfurling medium petals, look for the obvious gaps and start filling in. Again, make sure that these petals extend out ¼" as you glue around the center.

> **Set 5:** Apply twenty petals from Template: Dahlia 5. Continue to glue petals where there are gaps. If you have trouble seeing the gaps, turn the flower over and the gaps will be more visible. Pre-glue petals and hold the flower in your non-dominant hand so that you do not have to keep setting it down as you work.

> **Set 6:** Apply sixteen petals from Template: Dahlia 6. Continue gluing around the flower head to fill in gaps. At this point your flower is 4½" to 5" in diameter.

16. **To finish the foliage and stem,** put a line of tacky glue on the first bract strip, and attach it around the base. On the second time around, make sure that the bracts lay between the other bracts, filling in empty gaps.

17. Put lines of tacky glue on the six remaining bracts. Start by gluing three bracts in a triangle pattern for the first layer. Then apply the three remaining bracts in between the first layer. Wrap floral tape down the stem about 4". Attach the leaflet set to the main stem by wrapping with tape to secure. Wrap down the rest of the stem to finish.

Dahlia: Terracotta

Japanese Garden Rose: Miyabi

Create a stunningly beautiful garden rose with this detailed tutorial, inspired by the exquisite Miyabi Garden Rose from Wabara. "Miyabi" references the traditional Japanese aesthetic of elegance and refinement, beautifully embodied in this rose's soft ombre coloration and striking star-shaped center. In crafting this flower out of paper, you will master the art of employing two distinct coloring techniques and blending two different crepe weights to achieve a harmonious and lifelike appearance.

As one of the more intricate tutorials in this book, this rose will require patience and meticulousness, but the results will undoubtedly justify the time invested. Once you have mastered these techniques, you will have the skills to experiment with other color schemes and subtle variations in papers, allowing you to create an array of garden roses, each uniquely tailored to your artistic vision.

Japanese Garden Rose: Miyabi

German doublette crepe paper in leaf/moss

German doublette crepe paper light rose/pink

German doublette crepe paper in goldenrod/ buttercup

German doublette crepe paper in white/white

German extra fine crepe paper in blush

thirteen 9" 26-gauge wires for inner petals

one 18-gauge wire, for main stem

tacky glue

Mod Podge in matte

floral tape or Crepe Tape (page 24) in dark green

watercolor or gouache paint in red and white

soft pastel in yellow ocher, such as PanPastel 270.8 Yellow Ochre Tint

Tools: ruler, scissors, paintbrushes, wire cutter, makeup brush

2.

1. **For the matte-painted leaf paper,** cut one 9¾" x 3" strip and one 3¾" x 4" strip of leaf/ moss doublette crepe paper. Paint matte Mod Podge onto both strips. Let dry.

2. **For the pink ombre-painted petal paper,** cut two 12" x 10" sheets of light rose/pink doublette crepe paper; you will have extra for another rose project. Have a cup of water

ready to wet and clean your brush. Mix pools of watercolor: red, dark pink, lighter pink, and white. (Red and white make pink!) To paint an ombre effect on both sides of the pink strip, start with a wet brush to ready the paper, then add red along the long edge, and work up to pink and light pink, brushing to blend color transitions; mimic the same color pattern on both sides. (We will be cutting this strip into four long strips later, so use that measurement to gauge the color changes.) Let dry.

3. **For the stamens,** cut one 3" x 1" strip of goldenrod/buttercup doublette crepe. Fold in half against the grain, the lighter yellow (goldenrod) facing in. Cut one 3" x 2½" strip of white/white doublette crepe. Fringe about ¼" from the yellow edge to make a stamen as on page 19.

Note: The more pastel yellow you apply to the inner petal paper, the older the bloom will appear.

4. **For the inner petals,** cut against the grain to make eight 10" x 2" strips of German extra fine blush crepe. With a makeup brush, apply soft pastel in yellow ochre to both sides of all eight strips; it should not be perfectly blended, but rubbed in so no loose powder remains. Accordion fold all eight pastel-colored strips with the grain every 1¼" (sixty-four times). Cut the folds to make sixty-four pieces. Use Template: Miyabi 1 to cut them into sixty-four petals. Stretch the top fourth of each petal; go faster by stretching three or more at a time (a).

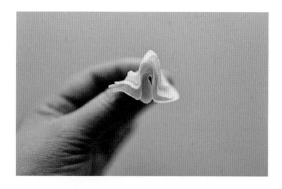

5. **To make sets of folded inner petals** (make eight sets consisting of eight petals in each set): Grab eight petals, put a dot of glue at the base of seven petals, and use the eighth unglued petal to start your petal gluing process. Fold each glue-dotted petal in half and layer it behind a glue-free petal such that each folded petal sits differently, peeking out up to ⅛" to the top, left, or right. Repeat for eight eight-petal sets. (Folding petal sets like this creates small air pockets so individual petals can be seen as you look at the rose's center.)

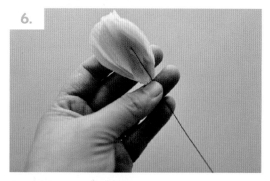

6. **To shape, wire the folded inner petal sets:** Put in a line of tacky glue halfway up the center of a folded inner petal set. Place one end of a 9" 26-gauge stem halfway up the petals and pinch the base of the petal set to secure it. Bend the base of the wire back about 45 degrees so the petals face up slightly. With an awl, curl the folded petal tops out and under, and curl the folded petal sides out and to the left and right. Repeat to make eight wired eight-petal sets.

7. **For the outer petals,** cut against the grain to make two 10" x 3" strips of ombre-painted light pink/rose crepe. Accordion fold both strips with the grain every 1⅔" (twelve times). Cut the folds to make twelve pieces. Use Template: Miyabi 2 to cut those pieces into twelve outer petals. Cut the remaining light pink/rose crepe into two 12" x 3" strips. Accordion fold both strips with the grain every 2" (twelve times). Cut the folds to make twelve pieces. Use Template: Miyabi 3 to cut them into twelve outer petals; be careful to

7

Japanese Garden Rose: Miyabi

8.

9a.

9b.

keep them separate from the Miyabi 2 petals, even as you complete the next steps. Cut a 1" slit into the middle of the base of all twenty-four. Put a dot of tacky glue to the right of the slit on a petal's base. Cross the left side of the base over and onto the glue on the right side of the base, forming an X and deeply cupping the shape. Repeat with the remaining outer petals. (Later, each X will hug the stem as you glue petals to the flower head.) Cup the base of each petal just above the X and slowly move up to make it more rounded and upright. Use an awl to tightly curl under the petals' left and right edges.

8. **For the calyx and leaves,** follow steps 10–13 for the Leonora Garden Rose (pages 160–162), but use a 9¾" x 3" strip to make five leaves. After assembling three of the leaves into a leaf set, floral tape down 1¾" and tape to attach the final two leaves opposite one another.

9. **To assemble,** brush to spread tacky glue evenly along the bottom half of the stamen strip. Wrap the stamen around the top of the 18-gauge wire (a). Apply tacky glue to the base of all eight eight-petal sets. Place them evenly around with their tops just above the stamens, and, before the tacky glue dries, shift and bend the petals' wires as you like (b).

Note: The more upright each petal sits, the more freshly bloomed the rose will be; the more bent back each petal sits, the older the rose will be. Adjust to perfectly age your rose.

10.

ROW 1

ROW 2

ROW 3

ROW 4

11.

10. **To attach the outer petals,** apply tacky glue to the base of all twenty-four petals. Attach the twelve lighter Miyabi 2 outer petals in layers.

> **Row 1:** Put the six lightest pink petals evenly around the stamen; they can overlap slightly, but it is not necessary.

> **Row 2:** Glue the six next lightest petals between the gaps. Attach the darker Miyabi 3 petals in rows.

> **Row 3:** Glue six petals between the gaps.

> **Row 4:** Glue the final six petals between the gaps. If your petals' curls are loose, you might need to tighten the curls by rolling it with your fingers.

11. **To finish the foliage and stem,** put a dot of tacky glue on each of the five calyxes and place them—equally spaced—around the base of the rose's head. Tape the bottom of the calyx and wrap tape down the main stem about 4". Wrap to secure the leaf set to the main stem. Wrap to the end to finish the stem.

Double Peony: Sarah Bernhardt

The double peony is cherished for its magnificent, dense, rounded shape, resulting from many layers of delicately ruffled petals and named after after the beautiful Sarah Bernhardt. Crafting such a lush and full paper peony is time-intensive, mirroring the care and attention needed to grow the live blooms that captivate so many gardeners and floral enthusiasts. Just as the fresh peonies stand out as showstoppers in gardens and floral arrangements with their opulent beauty, this paper replica demands patience and precision but is rewarding. The effort invested in creating this paper peony results in a breathtaking bloom that truly deserves to be the focal point of any arrangement. This project will challenge your crafting skills. Take your time to meticulously color and cut each petal before putting it together. I put together a petal tip guide to give you various creative ways to make each petal uniquely yours.

Double Peony: Sarah Bernhardt

German doublette crepe paper in leaf/moss

Italian crepe paper in 90 gsm 354 soft pink

German doublette crepe paper in white/white

one 18-gauge wire

two 26-gauge wires, cut in half for two 9" stems

spun cotton egg (25 mm x 20 mm)

tacky glue

floral tape or Crepe Tape (page 24) in medium green

Mod Podge in gloss

soft pastels in red, such as PanPastel 340.8 Permanent Red Tint

Tools: ruler, scissors, paintbrushes, wire cutters, awl

2. + 3.

BRACT

LEAVES

1. **To prepare Mod Podge-painted crepe,** cut against the grain to make one 7" x 3½" strip and one 6" x 3" strip of leaf/moss doublette crepe paper. Paint one side (the side you want seen) of each strip with gloss Mod Podge; for this peony, I prefer the lighter side (leaf), but it's up to you. Let dry.

Note: See Semi-Double Peony: Coral Charm (pages 139–140) for more how-to images of these leaves and bracts.

2. **For the leaves,** with the Mod Podge-painted side facing out, fold the 7" x 3½" strip of Mod Podge-painted leaf/moss doublette crepe in half twice until it is ¾" in width. Cut from corner to corner to get six triangle pieces. Seam miter six leaves as on page 22, wiring only three of the seven. Wire three of the leaves with the 26-gauge wires. Leave two unwired. Cut two

wired leaves from Template: Peony Leaf A and one wired leaf from Template: Peony Leaf B. Cut the three unwired leaves with Template: Peony Leaf A. Assemble a leaf set using the wired leaves. Start with Leaf B in the middle, add a wired Leaf A to the right, and another wired Leaf A slightly lower. Tape together and down about 2". Place the last Leaf A. Continue taping until no wires are exposed.

3. **For the bracts,** cut against the grain to make three with Template: Bracts A and three with Template: Bracts B out of the 6" x 3" strip of Mod Podge-painted leaf/moss doublette crepe. With the Mod Podge-painted side facing out, cup the top third of each bract until slightly concave.

4. **For the double petals,** cut against the grain to make one 25" x 3½" strip of soft pink crepe. Accordion fold with the grain every 1" (25 times). Cut the folds to make twenty-five 1" x 3½" pieces. Fold each piece in half with the grain (a). Place Template: Double Peony 1 over the fold to cut twenty-five double petals (b). Ruffle the tips and then deeply cup the double petals. Adjust the bottom petal slightly to the right, twisting each petal base to hold the two-petal set in a more opened layered position (c).

5. **For the 1" petals,** cut with the grain to make one 32" x 2½" strip of white/white doublette crepe. Accordion fold with the grain every 1" (thirty-two times). Cut the folds to make thirty-two pieces and use Template: Double Peony 2 to cut those pieces into thirty-two petals. Cut a variety of interesting edges into the 1" petals using the template as a guide.

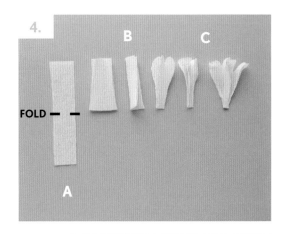

4.

B   C

FOLD – –

A

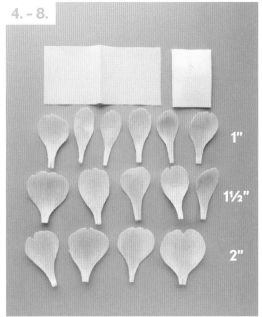

4. - 8.

1"

1½"

2"

6. **For the 1½" petals,** cut with the grain to make one 48" x 2½" strip of white/white doublette crepe. Accordion fold with the grain every 1½" (thirty-two times). Cut the folds to make thirty-two pieces and use Template: Double Peony 3 to cut them into thirty-two petals. Add interesting edges, again using the template as a guide for all the 1½" petals.

7. **For the 2" petals,** cut with the grain to make one 48" x 2½" strip of white/white doublette crepe. Accordion fold with the grain every 2" (twenty-four times). Cut the folds to make twenty-four pieces. Use Template: Double Peony 4 to cut them into twenty-four petals. Add interesting edges by again using the guide for all the 2" petals.

8. Brush red pastel to the bottom two-thirds of each petal, leaving the top one-third uncolored. Slightly cup and smooth each petal.

Note: When laminating paper, it's crucial to shape or manipulate it while the glue is still soft. The paper becomes highly malleable at this stage, allowing you to mold it into any desired shape. Once the glue sets and the paper dries, it becomes rigid, and any shaping becomes permanent. Therefore, working quickly and precisely during the lamination process is essential to achieve the desired shaping outcome.

9. **For the laminated petals,** cut with the grain to make nine 6" x 3" strips of white/white doublette crepe. Creasing each fold, accordion fold with the grain every 2" (three times). Laminate the three layers of each strip (as on page 20) to create nine 2" x 3" pieces. Cut four of the laminated pieces in half to make eight smaller pieces. Use Template: Double Peony 5 to cut those pieces into eight petals. Cut a ¾" wide strip off each of two of the remaining laminated pieces, for two more 1¼" pieces. Use Template: Double Peony 6 and 7 to cut them into petals. Cut the three remaining

laminated pieces into petals using Template: Double Peony 8. Cut texture into the tips of all thirteen laminated petals. Use a makeup brush to apply red-tint pastel to the bottom two-thirds of each petal, leaving the top third uncolored. Before the glue dries, stretch to smooth petals; stretch and smooth as much as you can without tearing the paper. Cut a ¾" slit into the center of each petal's base. (This makes it easier to glue them to the flower head.)

10.

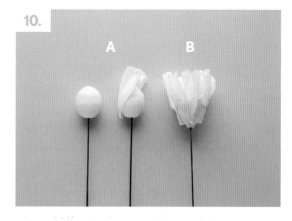

10. **For the core,** dot the premade hole in the spun cotton egg with tacky glue. Poke the end of the 18-gauge wire into the hole through the tacky glue (a). Dot tacky glue to apply four of the double petals around it, making sure the petal tops go about ¾" above the top of the core to cover it, forming the base of the flower head (b). Set aside to let dry.

11. **To attach petals to the flower head,** remember to avoid using too much glue. This big double peony blossom is so thick with petals (135 of them!) that even a little too much glue can make its flower head sag. One more tip: do not just glue the petals flat. Angle petals

11a.

11b.

11c.

into the gaps to create points of interest on the face of your peony. This is what makes the eye travel and how your peony can tell a story. To keep that story interesting, consider using the echoing technique—gluing a couple extra petals behind a lovely petal set that you want to accentuate. Put a small dot of glue on the base of all petal sets and single petals before attaching. Working in the following batches of petal sets, press to apply petals starting around the center and moving out toward the base of the flower head.

To make four petal sets, select three double petal strips and two 2" petals for each of the four sets. Put them together in varying combinations as follows:

For the first set, glue a double petal on top of a 2" petal with the double petal's top slightly lower. Glue another double petal strip slightly below the first. Glue the last double petal strip slightly below the second. Glue the last 2" petal to the right and behind the other 2" petal (a).

Repeat three more times for four five-petal sets. Take your time and fluff each of the petals. Make sure the tops closest to the center are ⅛" higher than the double petals already attached there (b).

To make five more petal sets, layer and (lightly!) tacky glue as you did the five-petal sets, but in the following combinations (c):

One set with one 2" petal and three double petal strips;

One set with one 2" petal and two 1½" petals;

Two sets with one 2" petal and one 1" petal; and

One set with one 1½" petal and one double petal strip.

12. Fluff those five petal sets and add them along with loose petals to the next layer around the center: five double petals, two 1" petals, four 1½" petals, and one 2" petal.

To make nine petal sets in varying combinations, lightly tacky glue the following evenly around the center:

Seven sets with two 1½" petals, slightly staggered;

Two sets with one 2" petal and one 1" petal.

13. **For the next petal sets,** make these combinations:

> **Three sets** with one 1½" petal and one 1" petal;
>
> **Four sets** with two 1½" petals;
>
> **Two sets** with one 2" petal and one 1" petal; and, last but not least,
>
> **one** loose 1" petal.

Note: Anytime you attach petals, remember to focus on the gaps; if you cannot see gaps, turn the flower upside-down and they will show. Use loose double petals to add volume and weight, and loose single petals to fill in space.

14. **To fill in the gaps,** fluff the remaining petal sets and tacky glue them into the gaps on the flower head. Then tacky glue the remaining seven 2" petals and twenty-one 1" petals into gaps, checking to make sure the peony's head is balanced all around. Push up the bottom of the petals so that they don't slide down the stem too far.

> **To attach the laminated petals,** tacky glue in the slim petals first, and then glue in the larger ones, saving the three largest laminated petals to add last of all.

15. **To finish the foliage and stem,** cut the plastic tube to the size of your stem; either use tacky glue or a glue gun to attach it to the base of your flower head. Let dry slightly. Glue the three pointed bracts spaced equally around the base. Add the round sepals in between the gaps. Go down about ½" to 1" from the sepals and glue the two unwired leaves flat to the stem. Floral tape one layer down the entire clear plastic tube to cover. With a pointed awl, poke a hole into the plastic tube about 4" down the stem from the flower head. Insert the leaflet set into the tube. Start from the top again and wrap floral tape down the entire stem. By floral taping several times, you cover any bumps and make the stem smoother. Slightly stretch and cup each of your bracts and leaves. Give it a bit of shape and movement by pinching the tips of the leaves and taking a moment to fluff the petals.

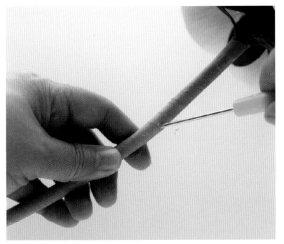

Double Peony: Sarah Bernhardt

FLORAL PROJECTS

YOU HAVE FLOWERS. WHAT'S NEXT?

Now it is time to play with the flowers that you made. Yes, putting your flower in a bud vase and calling it done is easy, but let's take it up a notch. I hope this section will give you the basics and kindle your floral design thirst for knowledge. One of the most important aspects of floral design is the composition of your bouquet, centerpiece, or installation. With paper florals, you control all of that! You have the ultimate say on how big or small the flower head is, the exact shade of green the leaves are, and how long those stems reach. Depending how much time you want to put into the flowers, you can be as elaborate and detailed as you want. To start a project, think about the color composition, the lines you want to create, and the overall form or story that you want to tell with your arrangement. All these aspects can be summed up in one important word: movement.

PAPER FLOWER MECHANICS: USING SHAPE, TEXTURE, AND COLOR TO CREATE MOVEMENT

Movement keeps the eye interested in an arrangement. It draws you in to discover more and more. Here's how you can do it.

Choose Colors: Create movement to your arrangements by playing around with colors. For example, make light to dark flowers and foliage, helping the eyes move from the light to the dark.

Create Lines: Place specific flowers in a fluid line so the eyes will follow it. Another way to create a line is by elongating stems so the flower head seems to float above the arrangement. Play with

symmetrical or asymmetrical arrangements. Don't be afraid to experiment. Wires can be added back onto stems if you cut too short. If you feel unsure, try a V line or soft S curve. They are easy shapes to replicate and pleasing to look at.

Vary Size and Stage: Create different sizes of blooms or the same type of blooms but in different blooming stages. This will keep everything from looking too uniform.

Play with Depth: Do not place all the flowers on the same plane of view. Consider placing a flower a little bit out and then tucking another bloom several inches down. This will help create depth and scale to your arrangement. Another way to create depth is making the same flower but in different shades of colors.

Add Texture: When creating your flowers, think about the different crepe papers and how you will use them to make different textures in your bouquets or arrangements. You can create textures by creating small clusters and bunches of flowers or multi-petal flowers. Coating your crepe with Mod Podge or acrylic paint will create another form of texture. Try making the same flower in a different crepe paper weight. The variation of paper thickness will also add a subtle difference.

Use Angles: Don't always put your flowers straight in the vase and facing forward. Arrange flowers so they angle, looking down or up and even looking at each other. It will seem like the flowers are conversing with each other.

Use Odd Numbers: How do you know how many flowers you want to make for your bouquet or arrangement? A simple rule of thumb is keeping your numbers odd like threes, fives, and sevens. It creates interest and contrast and disrupts patterns.

Embrace the Random: Avoid the temptation to use a grid or regular patterns to place your flowers. Nature is random, and that is what feels best to viewers. Also, never place two of the exact same flowers next to each other, or it looks like a pair of eyes staring at you, especially with a dark centered flower. Also avoid putting flowers in a polka dot pattern.

Choose a Vase: Sourcing the right vase to hold your flowers is the first step to arranging them. You have so many options: a simple bowl, an urn, a footed vase, multiple bud vases, a pitcher, a ginger jar, and more. And unlike regular flower arrangements, your vase does not have to be watertight! Your options are limitless if you want to put them in any vessel of your choosing.

When considering vases, consider the size of the blooms you want to use. Rule of thumb is the floral arrangement should be no more than 1½ times the width or height of the vase, otherwise the vase will be overwhelmed by the flowers or vice versa. With the right mechanics, the mouth of the vase will not be a problem for arranging your flowers. But do consider the weight of the flower heads and the size of your vase. Flowers that are too top heavy will fall over. You can easily fix this problem by adding weights like rice, beans, or rocks into the container. For wide, pedestal, or footed vases, using

mechanisms like floral tape or chicken wire will help you create elaborate shapes.

FLORAL MECHANICS

Floral mechanics refers to anything you use to help arrange your flowers or keep your flower in place. We are fortunate to have all our flowers and foliage made from wire, and you can bend or form whatever shape you can imagine. Besides just using the flowers' and foliage's wires, you can create beautiful pieces by making armatures out of wires or other natural materials such as curly willows—the possibilities are endless! With paper and wire armatures you can easily bend these materials into your bouquets or arrangements. I love that you are reusing them, and they are affordable, besides being quite easy to work with.

Chicken wire has long been a go-to choice for floral designers. You can use a small piece inside a vase to keep stems from slipping, and it is endlessly useful for larger pieces. You can easily find bulk rolls at home improvement or farming supply stores. I have also found that large crafting stores sometimes carry chicken wire coated in white and green plastic, but in smaller and more expensive quantities. When creating chicken wire armatures, roll the chicken wire to create a multi-layer cylindrical piece that can support the floral and foliage stems as you insert them. Make sure to tuck the pointy edges of the chicken wire toward the middle of the armature. I try to create a minimum of three layers depending on the vase vessels or large installations. Usually, these chicken wires are meant to be hidden and not seen. But you can also design these wire structures to be a statement piece that helps elevate your art piece. You can keep the chicken wire in place with clear floral tape. Once you have your chicken wire in place, take your floral tape and tape a nine-grid tape over to secure the tape in place. Wrap your clear floral tape at the edge of the vase's exterior to hold it in place.

For wedding bouquets, I like to use binding wires or craft covered 18- or 16-gauge wires to make a lightweight armature that helps hold the flowers in place. These armatures will help create a light and airy bouquet and help create spaces or small pockets of air in between the flowers. The armature mechanics can help you manipulate, guide, and hold the flowers in place. When arranging flowers in a vase, I like to start with a heavy flower frog, commonly known as kenzan, made of either heavy brass or a lead base held in place by floral putty. Then I make a chicken wire pillow and tape it down with clear floral tape to hold everything together. Using mechanics like this, you can use more wide and varied vases, instead of limiting yourself to vases with a narrow neck. When using flower frogs, make sure your wire stem is thick enough to hold onto the flower frog. Heavier flowers like peonies and tulips with the clear tubing stems are easier to insert, and having the chicken wires above will help hold the thinner stems in place along with the clear floral tape holding down the chicken wire pillow. Floral frogs come in many different shapes and materials, from ceramics to glass to wire hairpins, but the most well-known are the metal pins.

Tip: *When considering and making your own floral mechanics, you have a wide range of color options. Consider using white floral cloth wires to create your armature when using a white vase, or if you have a dark vase, consider wrapping your wires in dark crepe paper to make your mechanics less visible.*

Floral Headpiece

I love this project because even the tiniest flowers can take center stage when you create an airy and delicate headpiece. It is a fun way to showcase your paper flowers for a garden soiree, a bridal shower, or a birthday party. Don't be afraid to use bigger flowers if you like—just make sure they are proportionate to the face. Here I use a lightweight brass headband as the base, but any simple, clean headband will do.

Note: If you have light-colored hair, use white or gold wires. If you have dark-colored hair, use the dark green wires. Using the proper wire color will help it almost disappear in the background. Wire length will vary depending on how long you want each tendril to be.

1. **To prepare the flowers:** Make sure your chamomile flowers have around ½" stems or less. Keeping the stems short gives the illusion that the flower heads are so light and airy that they (seem to!) float.

2. **For the structure,** wrap one end of a 12" wire once around a marker (or similar object) to make a small, ½" circle just wide enough for a short flower stem to be inserted later—not so wide that it slips through. Make another circle about 1½" to 2" down the wire from the first. Repeat that to make three or four total (depending on your spacing) and leave 2" to 3" bare at the end so you can attach it to the headband. Repeat to make a total of two 12"

wires with three to four circles each, three 15" wires with five to six circles each, and three 18" wires with seven to eight circles each.

3. **To attach the flowers,** use a glue gun to adhere forty-two of the chamomile flower heads onto the forty-two circles. Then, to add the remaining chamomile flower heads, wrap each one's ½" stem with a 2" stem wire, going around the base a couple of times and then twisting it tight. Twist to secure some of these stemmed chamomile flowers at the side of the headpiece and some randomly around the flower wires. Attaching these flowers at random will help you fill in any empty spots around the headpiece.

4. Cut extra 2" pieces of 30-gauge wire as needed to tie the 22-gauge wire flower stems onto the headband. Use needle-nose pliers to twist each one tightly at the base, so the stem is on tight. Trim off any excess wire to keep your piece tidy.

5. **To shape the floating flower heads,** I like to create S-curve lines with flower groupings. Think about what viewers will look at first in a piece and how their eyes will travel to see the whole arrangement. Each head is different, and so is every flower. Go with what works best visually for your piece.

6. **Check the weight.** If the piece is too heavy on one side and causing flowers to droop, readjust the components until the flowers stay in place. Walk around the house to test out the piece. Jump up and down in front of the mirror to see how the headpiece holds up. Have fun!

Note: Not only are real flowers ephemeral and short-lived, some of them are also toxic to humans and pets. Floral Headpieces can be a safer alternative for parties and photo outfits. (Of course, they are for decoration only and no pet should be left alone with them; use your own best judgment.)

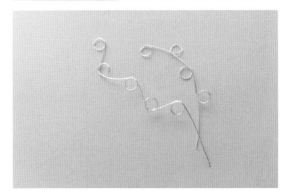

Floral Wear

Display your paper flowers with a wearable arrangement that can adhere to skin or clothes like an ethereal floral tattoo, inspired by Sue McLeary, an American floral designer. You can also use this technique to create modern boutonnieres and corsages and to add florals to shoes. Let your imagination run wild! This arm piece uses the Italian Butterfly Ranunculus (page 62) in shades of pink and assorted sizes. But you can use any flower you like.

You can get creative with greenery, too. If you want foliage, choose small, delicate looking leaves, and wire them as on page 23. Wiring foliage gives you more control of how it lays on and moves with the body. Stemless flowers and foliage work well for a close-to-the body look. Alternatively, you can put a short stem on each flower and leaf to create airy and whimsical pieces that float above the skin.

crepe paper flowers of your choice, ranging in sizes

foliage of your choice, if desired

athletic tape, nude for skin or to match clothing

Tools: glue gun, scissors

1. **Decide on placement.** For this tutorial, I show you how to put a large piece on your arm, plus several small pieces on your shoulder and hand.

2. **Prepare the tape.** Without removing the athletic tape's sticker backing, place it on your arm (or wherever you want it) to measure, and cut it slightly longer than your arm (or other area). Depending on how you want the floral wear to look and where you place it, you may want to taper cut one or both ends for a delicate look.

3. **Arrange flowers and foliage** on athletic tape. Play around and find an arrangement that is pleasing to your eye. Think of the lines and colors you are creating with the flowers and foliage. Attach flowers and foliage with a glue gun; use buds or foliage to fill in any spots where you can still see tape. Gently bend the tape to find any gaps that show with movement. If there are gaps, glue in small flowers or leaves to cover them. Remember, your floral wear will shift and move around when worn. If desired, use a glue gun to put individual flowers or buds onto ½" circles of athletic tape for smaller side pieces to wear as accents to your main piece.

4. **To wear,** gently peel off the tape backing, and place floral wear as desired.

5. **Adjust and rearrange as needed.** Because you made your floral wear out of paper, you can trim any pieces that do not lay or look as you envisioned. Add extra pieces as needed. Have fun and be creative. Peel and stick athletic tape to adhere flowers anywhere you want.

Mini Floral Wear: Glue gun individual flowers or buds onto ½" circles of athletic tape. To wear, gently peel off the tape backing and place as desired.

Heart-Shaped Bridal Bouquet

Putting together a hand-tied bouquet for a bride can be tricky—but using the correct floral mechanics can make it easier. A wire bouquet armature helps hold flowers in place and creates little pockets of space in all the right places. I make this bouquet's armature in the same green as the stems, so they blend. All it takes is about two wires to make, nothing too big or complicated.

Use simple flowers to balance out multi-petaled ones like the double peony, zinnia, and garden rose. The stephanotis and Italian butterfly ranunculus are good flowers for adding a different texture and size into the arrangement. You can use the flowers described in this tutorial to make the bouquet as shown or follow along with flowers of your own choosing.

Make sure all the foliage and flowers have long, uncut stems so you can pull and rearrange each piece before trimming the ends. (Of course, it is so easy to build out a stem with another wire if it is not long enough for its ideal placement.)

Always ask the bride her height and size so you can build the bouquet to fit her physique.

And keep in mind there is always a front and a back; you want to make sure the back of the bouquet lays flat as she will be holding it against her body. One small note: My bridal clients always tell me that I can put any flowers I want in the bouquet, but there is usually one flower that is special to them. One special thing that I do for each bride is nestling her favorite flower in the back so when she is looking down at her bouquet, she will be looking at her special flower that no one else will see but her.

Heart-Shaped Bridal Bouquet

two kraft-covered wires in green, for an armature, optional

two of the Double Peony (page 210)

seven of the Italian Butterfly Ranunculus (page 62) in yellow

four of the Zinnia (page 182)

one of the Lilac Sprig (page 78)

two Stephanotis (page 42) with foliage

three of the English Garden Rose: Leonora (page 156)

two of the Japanese Garden Rose: Miyabi (page 200)

eight of the Spray Rose: Princess Fairy Kiss (page 98) in pink

one silk ribbon in cream or color of choice

1. **For the armature,** if desired: Use two kraft-covered wires to build out a small armature. Start by making an oval shape with one wire, about 3½" in diameter. Weave the other wire around the oval shape, making 1" holes. This gives you a lot of places to insert stems and keep them in place.

2. **Consider the base shape.** For this project, I know I want to create a heart-shaped bouquet for the bride to hold. I keep this shape in

my mind as I build out the piece. The bride requested the pink double peony and a pink Miyabi garden rose as her favorite flowers. She wanted a happy, summery bouquet. I think about this while choosing the flowers and colors to support these main flowers.

3. **Place the flowers, starting with the focal flower,** which is either the largest or most important one—in this case, the double peony. I place it low and center. The second peony I place high and to the left. This creates a line that I know I want my viewer to see. To build out that line, I place one of the Miyabi roses to the right of the double peony and then another one to the right of the second peony, slightly lower than the double peony. Add the lilac stem under the left double peony. I take the other purple poppy and tuck it under the right side of the Miyabi garden rose. The zinnias come

next; the heavy, multi-petal flowers will appear lighter when zinnias extend the shape. Add three zinnias to the right side, framing out the heart-shaped bouquet. Place the fourth zinnia to the left side underneath the left double peony and to the left of the lilac. To fill in the left side of the bouquet, place eight spray roses into the left bottom side and back. To break up the pinkness of the bouquet, add stephanotis to the right of the bottom center double peony and then top left of the center double peony. The seven yellow Italian butterfly ranunculus help break up the pink and add lightness. The yellow petals of the ranunculus help highlight the centers of the zinnias. Place one ranunculus to the left, floating above the lilac stem, and then place a second ranunculus underneath and to the right of the floating ranunculus. Place five more ranunculus to create a soft S curve to the left so the eye follows the ranunculus to the left and then they carry the story to the right of the bouquet. Insert the last three garden roses to fill any gaps and make sure the viewer will see the heart shape.

Note: Consider using a floor mirror to better see the bouquet while you work. Check for any dark holes and either shift the flowers or add one to fill.

4. **To finish a bouquet,** use 3" to 4" floral tape to bind all the stems. This will keep them from shifting as you tie the ribbon to finish the bouquet; start the ribbon right under the armature and tie a knot to secure it to the bouquet. Trim all the stems so they are nice and even.

Note: I do not use too much greenery in this bridal bouquet. The choice is yours to add as much or little as you like. Foliage can play both a primary and secondary role, depending on where you place it. Long greenery can also help you create long lines in an arrangement, much like the zinnias do here.

Short Modern Monochromatic Floral Arrangement

I love monochromatic arrangements where either the flowers are all the same color, or the entire arrangement is one type of flower and the same color. The English floral designer Joseph Massie truly inspired me. If you are not following him, please do. You will learn so much from his teachings. Monochromatic arrangements do not just mean using just one color. Explore the different shades, hues, or tints/tones of a particular color. Consider creating a watercolor palette with just one base color and a pool of white and black to adjust it into a variety of shades that all work together.

The Double Cherry Blossom Branch is resplendent with monochromatic color. Use it in this project to make a small arrangement for the coffee table or your bedside table in a short amount of time. (If you want something grander and have a bit more time, see Project 5, page 242, for a large-scale three-foot cherry blossom display piece that you can put in a vase or hang on the wall.)

Short Modern Monochromatic Floral Arrangement

nine short Double Cherry Blossom Branches (page 142), each about 9" long with five to nine blossoms

Note: *Make sure the cherry blossom stems have about 4" to 5" of bare branches to be able to insert or tuck into the other branches.*

one long Double Cherry Blossom Branch, about 12" long with twenty to twenty-four blossoms

vase or vessel of choice

clear floral tape

kenzan (flower pin frog)

floral putty

chicken wire

Tools: ruler, scissors, wire cutter, needle-nose pliers, awl

Tip: *With a lower vase, even a narrow mouthed one, you may need additional mechanics to hold the flowers in place. I recommend taping a 9-grid formation at the mouth with clear floral tape. For wider openings, I use a 12-grid as well as chicken wire, a pin frog, and clear floral tape. See page 223–224 for more information about floral mechanics.*

1. **Prepare the vase.** Take a small amount of floral putty and attach it to the bottom of your metal pin frog. Stick it in the middle of your composition. Cut a square piece of chicken wire about 8" x 8". Form a multi-layer pillow and place it on top of the pin frog. Push the chicken wire down so it is level with the vase lip. Tape down the chicken wire with clear floral tape—I use between eight to twelve pieces. It is extra reinforcement to help hold the floral stems upright.

2. **Consider the base shape.** I love arrangements with an abstract V shape with one side lower than the other. It at once creates a beautiful line that the eye can follow and creates a story that anyone will see right away. When creating this arrangement, keep this V shape in mind. Start by inserting the long 12" branch to the right side of the vase at an angle. Take one of the 9" branches and insert to the left of the vase. Take the other eight branches and build out the shape. If you want your pieces taller, carefully insert the branch at the top.

3. **Use vase mechanics** to make the arrangement lusher. Build out the center and make sure to place the branches at an angle to build out your arrangement. Cover all the branches so you do not see them. It will make your arrangement all that lusher and more decadent. Check the view from all around the arrangement if it will be seen from different angles.

Tall Monochromatic Floral Arrangement

Scale up for a tall and striking composition. This arrangement builds on techniques used in Project 4 with added techniques for creating the weight, shape, and movement necessary for a large statement piece. With this project, a tall Double Cherry Blossom Branch gets the added beauty of age, with weight, knobs, and texture thanks to wire work and a papier-mâché of scrap crepe paper.

For this piece, follow the rule that the flowers can be up to 1½ times taller than the vase. Large arrangements require large components. But this piece does not have to go into a vase. Consider putting it in an unconventional vessel or hanging it on the wall or like a chandelier over your dining table. (For hanging piece instructions, see page 245.)

Tall Monochromatic Floral Arrangement

195 Double Cherry Blossom Branches (page 142), about 3' long with about sixty-five small branches with three to nine blossoms per branch

tall vase

clear floral tape

white crepe paper, any kind

tacky glue

at least twelve 18-gauge wires

Tools: ruler, scissors, needle-nose pliers, wire cutters

1. **Start with** a small three-blossom branch and start taping and attaching another small branch to this one. You can use glue to attach it together and then start taping it up. Use the ends of the branches to create knobs and interesting texture to your branch. Use the same method you would use to attach the blossom clusters as on page 149.

2. **To age the main branch,** twist the ends of the blossom wires around the main branch. Using the papier-mâché technique, cover crepe scraps with tacky glue and apply them onto the branch with a flat brush to build up and mold the shape. Keep measuring and comparing the branch to the vase to make sure you are making the branch long enough and building out the shape you want for the arrangement; also, check that your branch's diameter does not exceed that of the vase's opening (if using one). Wrap to add wires, tacky glue, and layers of crepe scraps as needed to lengthen and shape the branch; use heavier wires at the base of the branch for weight, bulk, and stability. Stop when you are satisfied with the shape.

3. **For the textured bark,** bulk up your main stem with crepe paper scraps. You can cut them into strips or glue on large rectangle pieces to bulk up your branch. Your aim is to smooth out the texture but at the same time emphasize the wire knobs on the branch.

4. **To style,** floral tape your piece and place it into your chosen vase. Depending on your vase and the width of the stem, you can use the clear floral tape to create a grid to narrow the vase neck. This will keep the branch upright or tilted the way you want to display your branch. Fluff up individual blossoms and bend and move the individual branches to your liking. Make sure some blossoms are facing toward the viewer and some are looking away.

Note: To preserve your paper florals, give them a good shake or use an air sprayer to remove the dust, and then occasionally spray with UV spray to preserve the color.

Hanging Tall Monochromatic Floral Arrangement: In step 2, pause while taping up the branch, find an optimum place where the branch will hang where you want, and bend one of the 18-gauge wires to create a hook. Make sure to hide the hook around some blossoms. It's always important to hide your mechanics.

Note: Keep practicing. Play with your flowers. The more you make flowers, the better you will get. Creativity comes from playing and creating and letting your imagination run wild! Eventually you will find your style, but if you have not found it yet, keep learning and making, because the more you practice, the easier it will become!

PROJECT TEMPLATES

Here you will find templates for a variety of shapes needed to make crepe paper flowers. Unless you are comfortable using these templates for visual reference and freehand cutting your own shapes, you will need to trace and transfer the templates to create traceable patterns.

Here's how: To make a pattern, hold or tape tracing paper (or parchment paper, or any other translucent or transparent paper) over a template. Trace around the border with a pencil. Note the grain direction and any dart marks. Use scissors to cut out the shape. Trim around the edges and corners to clean them up if needed. Now you can transfer the template onto crepe paper as many times as you need; simply place the template pattern on top of the crepe, checking that the paper grain is going in the right direction as marked. Hold the template pattern in place while you trace lightly around it in pencil. Cut along the pencil lines with scissors. Gently erase any pencil lines.

If you want to extend the life of the template patterns you make, try this hack: Use clear shipping tape to cover both sides, and then trim off excess tape. Template patterns encased in tape are stiffer, more durable, and easier to trace. They are hard to rip or tear.

Once you trace and cut out your template patterns, label each one to make reusing them a breeze. Store labeled patterns for later use.

Note: *If you have trouble cutting tiny petals, it is OK to cut them slightly larger than what the template shows. Getting the exact petal shape is more important than the precise sizing. Once you get more proficient, cut them smaller and to size.*

Sweet Pea: Raspberry Flake

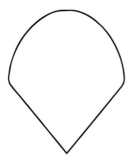

Petal

Lg. Leaf

Sm. Leaf

Pansy

Petal 2

Petal 1

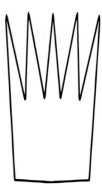

Sepal

Stephanotis

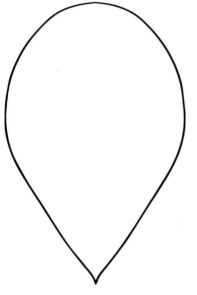

Leaf

Petal 1

Petal 2

Calyx

Bud

Ranunculus

Petal 1

Petal 2

Petal 3

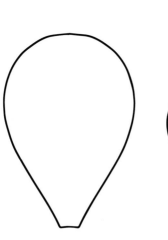

Petal 4

Sepal

Leaf

Italian Butterfly Ranunculus

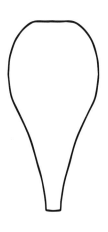

Petal 1

Leaf 1

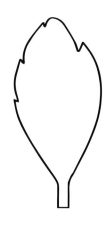

Leaf 2

Sepal

Foxglove

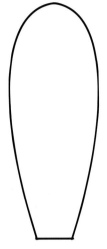

Top Petal

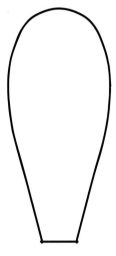

Bottom Petal

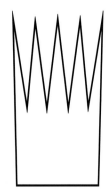

Sepal

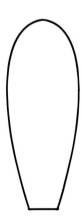

Bud Top

Bud Bottom

Lilac Sprig: Purple Sensation

Petal

Chamomile Flower

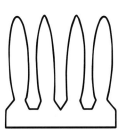

Petal

Leaf

Night Blooming Cereus or Hoa Quynh

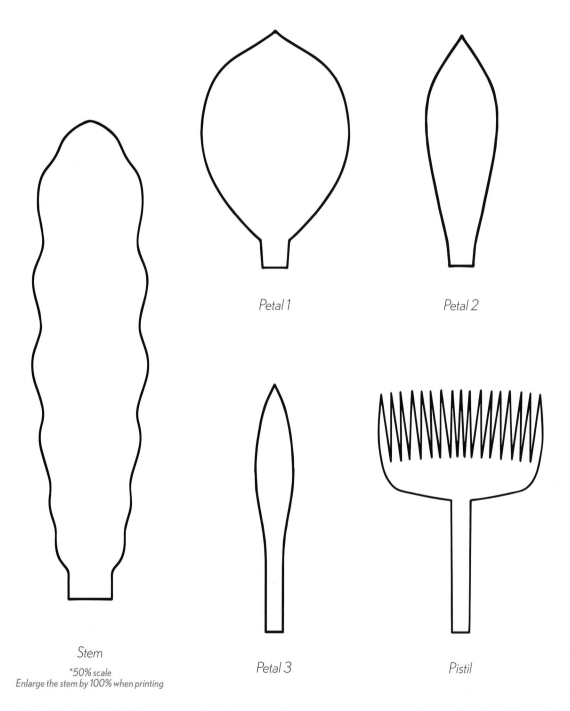

Petal 1

Petal 2

Stem
*50% scale
Enlarge the stem by 100% when printing*

Petal 3

Pistil

THE NEW ART OF PAPER FLOWERS

Spray Rose: Princess Fairy Kiss

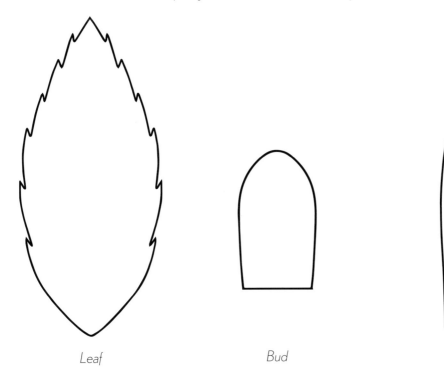

Leaf

Bud

Calyx

Petal 1

Petal 2

Poppy: Amazing Gray

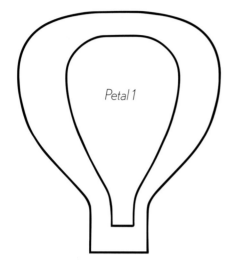

Petal 1

Petal 2

Icelandic Poppy

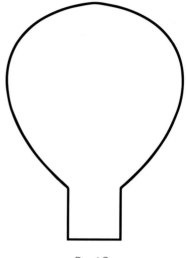

Petal 2

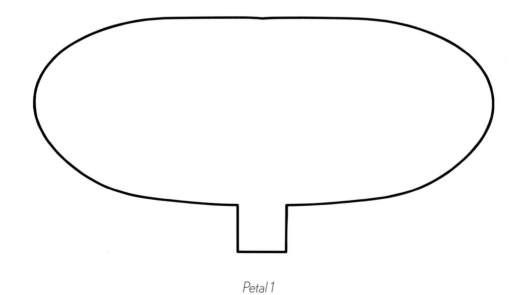

Petal 1

Single Peony: Claire de Lune

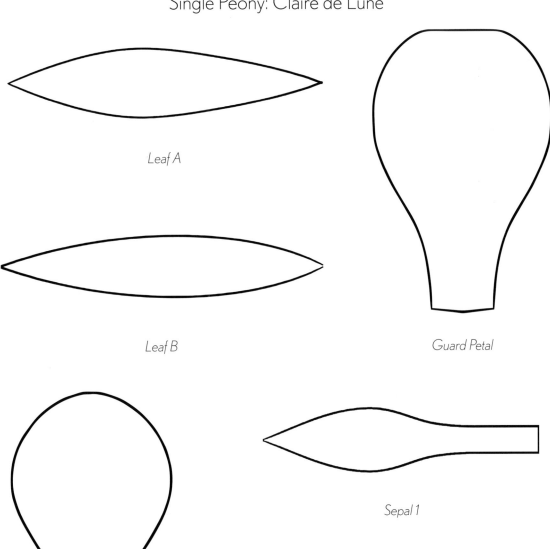

Leaf A

Leaf B

Guard Petal

Large Petal

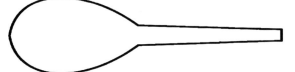

Sepal 1

Sepal 2

Semi-Double Peony: Coral Charm

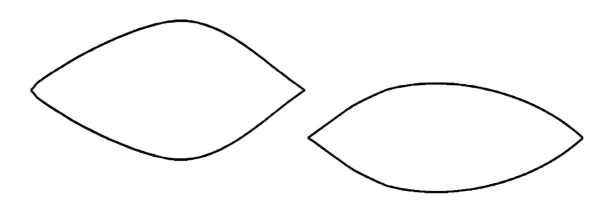

Leaf A   *Leaf B*

THE NEW ART OF PAPER FLOWERS

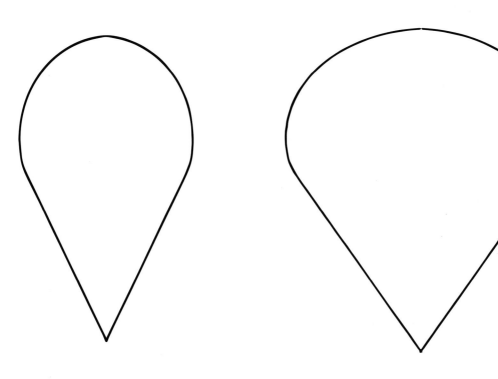

Petal 1   *Petal 2*

Double Cherry Blossom Branch

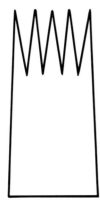

Sepal

Petal

Clematis

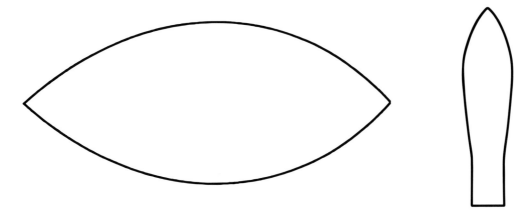

Petal

Stamen

English Garden Rose: Leonora

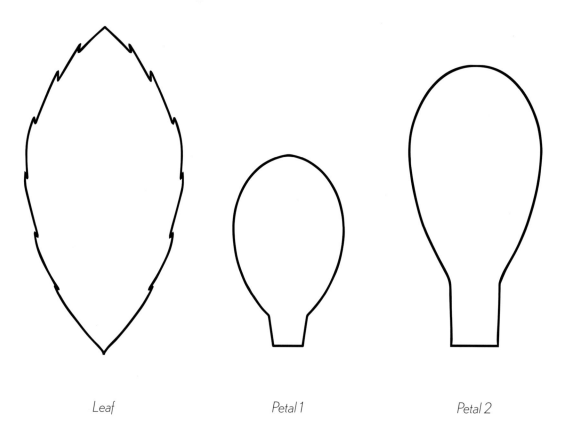

Leaf

Petal 1

Petal 2

Calyx

Tulip

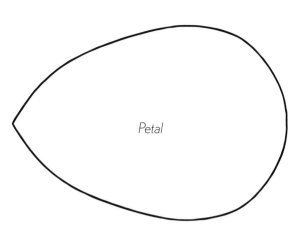

Petal

Peony Tulip

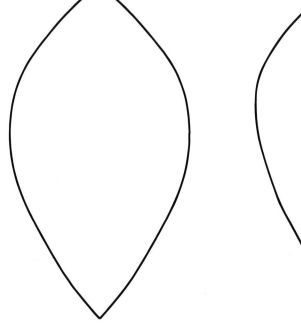

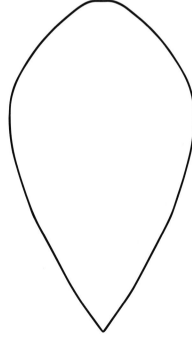

Petal 1   *Petal 2*

Petal 1

Petal 2

Petal 3

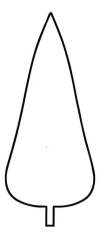

Leaf

Dahlia

Petal 1

Petal 2

Petal 3

Petal 4

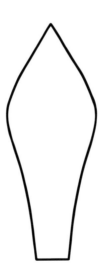

Petal 5

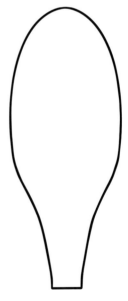

Petal 6

Project Templates

Dahlia

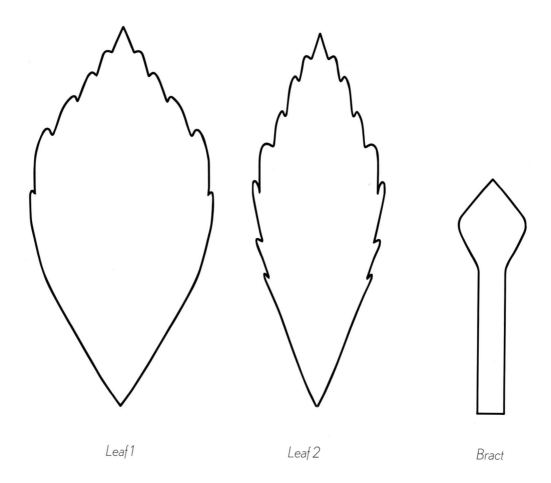

Leaf 1   *Leaf 2*   *Bract*

Japanese Garden Rose: Miyabi

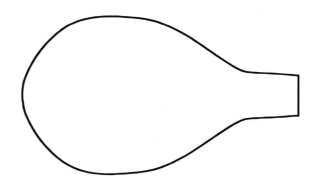

Petal 1

Petal 2

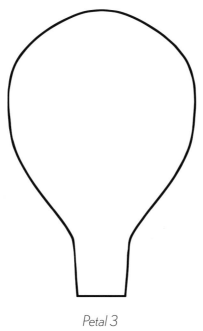

Petal 3

Double Peony

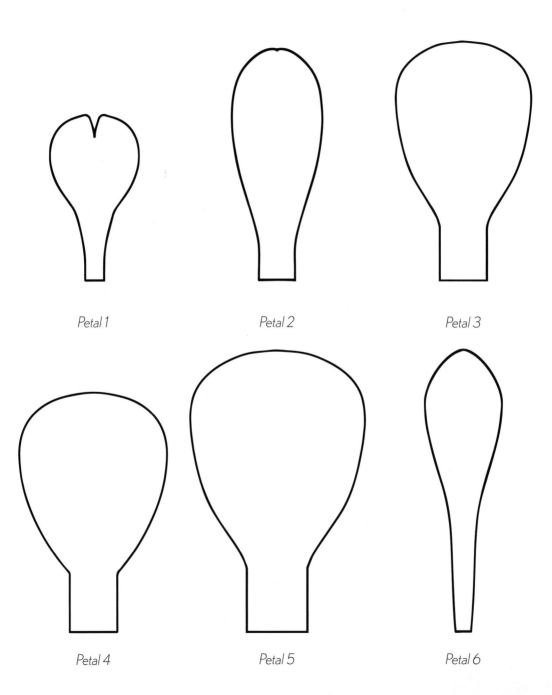

Petal 1

Petal 2

Petal 3

Petal 4

Petal 5

Petal 6

Double Peony

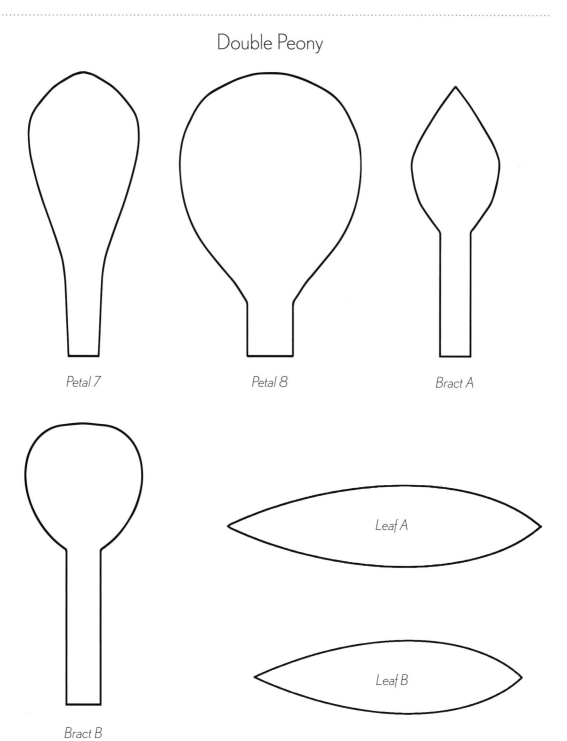

Petal 7

Petal 8

Bract A

Bract B

Leaf A

Leaf B

Conversion Chart for International Measurements

$1/_{16}$" = approximately 1.59 mm

$1/_8$" = approximately 3.18 mm

$7/_8$" = approximately 22.23 mm

¼" = approximately 6.35 mm

1" = approximately 25.4 mm

1½" = approximately 38.1 mm

2" = approximately 50.8 mm

2½" = approximately 63.5 mm

3" = approximately 76.2 mm

1 mm ≈ $1/_{25}$ inch

2 mm ≈ $1/_{12}$ inch

3 mm ≈ $1/_8$ inch

4 mm ≈ $1/_8$ inch

5 mm ≈ $3/_{16}$ inch

6 mm ≈ ¼ inch

7 mm ≈ $9/_{32}$ inch

8 mm ≈ $5/_{16}$ inch

9 mm ≈ $11/_{32}$ inch

10 mm ≈ $13/_{32}$ inch

11 mm ≈ $7/_{16}$ inch

12 mm ≈ ½ inch

ACKNOWLEDGMENTS

I am forever grateful to my family and friends who have supported me in my paper flower journey, including my sweet husband, Daniel, and my fur baby, Butter. Without their support and patience, I could not have met my deadline while I wrote and photographed all the tutorials. Thank you to my mother and father, my sisters, Tran and Kim, and my little brother, Don, for their constant support and encouragement, and most of all, for believing that I could do this.

My love of paper flowers grew because of my online family of paper flower enthusiasts and makers. I found a community of people who could relate to my paper flower tribulations. Many thanks to Jessie Chui, Sara Kim, Ann Wood, and others for your support and cheering.

Thank you to Yvonne Wong for capturing the vision I was trying to achieve with my paper flowers for the project section, making them more modern, but giving them a soft and airy look.

Thank you so much to my publishing team at Blue Star Press. You made this book process so seamless and wonderful. Special thanks to Avalon Radys, Margaret McGuire Novak, Lindsay Wilkes-Edrington, Bryce de Flamand, Bailey Dueitt, and Peter Licalzi for giving me this chance to share my paper flower love with the world.

Thank you to Sarah Simon for sharing her vision and creativity with me. Her passion for teaching has pushed me to extend my painting knowledge.

Many thanks to Alexandra Farms, especially Joey Azout and Teresa Schafer, for sharing their garden rose passion with me. It was amazing to visit their beautiful Garden Rose Farm in Colombia and see all the lovely garden roses in person. And special thanks to the David Austin team for giving me permission to share the Leonora Garden Rose in the book.

Thanks to Cartotecnica Rossi, Werola, Carte Fini, and Rose Mille for creating and providing such beautiful crepe paper. Without them, I would not have started my paper flower journey.

I could not have done this book without support from Kelsey Reed, Jerry Kear, Vikki Nakamura, Myra Tanita, Megan O'Brien, Kasia Puszkiewicz, Joanna Derengowska, Alicia Schwede, and Gisela Santos. Thank you to all my friends around the world who believed in me and knew I could make this book happen.

The English Garden Rose: Leonora (page 156)
is inspired by Leonora (Auswagsy) with
permission from David Austin Wedding Roses.

Photography, text, and tutorials by Quynh D. Nguyen
@pinkandposey

Photography on pages 225–243 by Yvonne Wong

ISBN 9781958803783

Printed in Colombia

Cover design by Bryce de Flamand
Design by Bryce de Flamand

10 9 8 7 6 5 4 3 2 1

ABOUT THE AUTHOR

Quynh D. Nguyen is the paper artist behind Pink and Posey's stunning fine art installations. Drawing on her extensive experience and educational background in marketing and finance, her goal is to empower others wherever they may be on their creative journey. She shares her knowledge about entrepreneurship and paper flower artistry through speaking engagements, workshops, online classes from The Posey Box, and co-hosting *Paper Talk*™ *Podcast*. Her work has been featured in numerous media outlets, both nationally and locally in the Seattle area. Learn more at pinkandposey.com.